"The Way I Heard It"

A Three Nation
Reading Vacation

2nd Edition

Arnie Marchand

The stories that were told to the author and those that have been passed down for generations of Okanogan Indians, interviews with a variety of individuals and excepts from noted works about areas of Indian country between Wenatchee, WA and Enderby, BC to the North.

Photography:
        The information below indicates ownerships of the photo and drawings in the book.

ANM	Arnie Marchand
OBHS	Okanogan Borderlands Historical Society
HP	Heritage Productions
PB	Public Domain
C&E	Cates & Erb, Inc.

To order additional copies of this book, contact the publishers:

Heritage Productions
PO Box 909
Oroville, WA 98844
email: heritageproductions@gmail.com

Okanagan Nation Alliance

OKANAGAN
INDIAN BAND

OSOYOOS
INDIAN BAND

UPPER SIMILKAMEEN
INDIAN BAND

PENTICTON
INDIAN BAND

WESTBANK FIRST NATION

UPPER NICOLA
INDIAN BAND

LOWER SIMILKAMEEN
INDIAN BAND

The Confederated Tribes of the Colville Reservation covers 1.4 million acres in North Central region of the State of Washington and is a Sovereign Nation.

The 10 original tribes were Nespelem, San Poil, Chelan, Wenatchi, Entiat, Methow, Southern Okanogan, Moses-Columbia, Methow, Sweel-Too (Colville).

These tribes were joined by the Palus and Chief Joseph's band of the Nez Perce.

Foreword

The previous pages have the symbols of the seven bands of the Okanagan Indians of British Columbia. The Confederated Tribes of the Colville Reservation in Washington State consists of 10 original bands which all spoke Nsyilxcn, the Okanogan language. The stories are a part of the history, custom and culture of the area called Indian Country. There were two tribes added to our reservation in the 1880's, the Palus and the Nez Perce and today there are 12 tribes of the Confederated Tribes of the Colville Reservation.

The people and organizations that helped me in completing this piece of work were Mike and Kay Sibley, Wilbur G. (Web) Hallauer, Cayle Diefenbach, Wendell George, Black Horse Productions owned by Bill Black, David Lindeblad, and Thelma Achmire the En'owkin Centre on the Penticton Indian Reserve near Penticton, the Okanogan County Historical Society, Okanogan Borderlands Historical Society, the Wenatchee Valley College Library at Omak, the Wenatchee Museum and Cultural Center, the Upper Columbia Museum Association, and the friends and relatives who put up with me.

If I have forgotten anyone or an organization I am truly sorry. It is an oversight not an attempt to slight you, age does that!

Arnie Marchand HP

It is traditional to introduce myself in this manner.

My father is George Paul Marchand, from the Okanagan Indian Band #1. My mother is Sophie Alice Verdan Marchand from the Penticton Indian Band. I am an Okanagan Indian and Member of the Confederated Tribes of the Colville Reservation, my Indian name is ML KNOOPS, (meaning Eagle), my Christian name is Arnold N. Marchand.

It is an honor to have you read some of these stories on your way through the traditional territories of the Okanagan Indian People. Thank you.

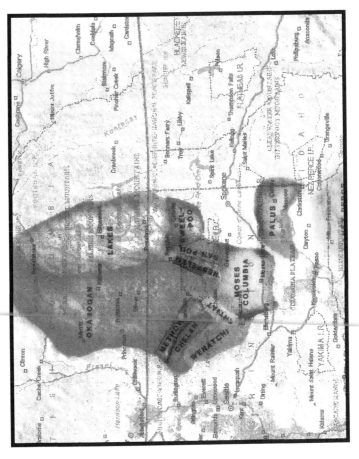

Indian Country   ANM

A Three Nation Vacation

You know that some Indian People can tell Indian stories so eloquently, you seem to be there and are engulfed in the story of Animal People, Coyote, or the Ancient Ones. They take you back into history and retell the story of Indian People as if you were there.

I, on the other hand, tell stories about Indians; stories about my People, the Okanogan Indians, and the people that lived in the traditional territories of my People.

I want you to take a Three Nation Vacation with me through my traditional territory that will begin in Wenatchee, North Central Washington, and end near Enderby in lower British Columbia, and it is all Indian Country.

When the first contact was made, the white man asked "what is your country, where are your boundaries, where are your borders?" The Okanogan leaders had a great deal of difficulty with that concept. We did not think in terms of borders or boundaries. Countries and territories were not strange to us but we did not know how to answer. An elder stood up after long deliberation and said "Our territory ends where our tongue ends."

To the North with the Shu Shwap Indians, to the East the Kootenai and Flathead and the Spokane and to the South the Yakama and the West is bordered by the mountains, this is our traditional country.

If you don't know the answer, ask someone older and generally they know how to answer the question. If you listen long enough you will learn more than when you are talking. Remember to ask your elders. Talk to your people (relatives), ask about your history, your custom, culture and tradition. No school, no college, no university will answer these questions better than your own People. The People of the Confederated Tribes of the Colville Reservation and the Seven Bands of the Okanagan People have many who are wise beyond their years and elders that can help answer your questions about our People. Remember, no question is a stupid question and the only stupid question is the one you didn't ask. And so, we learn this lesson about Indian Country.

I want you to know something about the People of the Okanogan's traditional territory. I will begin by telling you something about who we are and how we lived.

We lived in pit houses and Tule mat lodges, (BC) before Caucasians in the 1800's. The pit houses were from waist deep to shoulder deep with logs forming the roof. Both the Tule mat lodge and pit house will be described later in this book.

We are a Salmon People and much of our custom, culture and tradition revolved around the Salmon. The Salmon stopped at four places in our traditional territory, a place now called Enloe Dam on the Similkameen River near Oroville, Washington, Okanagan Falls in British Columbia, Kettle Falls near Colville, Washington, and Spokane Falls in Spokane, Washington. These are

Salmon jumping at the falls   NCW

the places that the Salmon would be unable to travel any further.

These fisheries were gathering places of great importance and protocol, where many tribes gathered.

The Salmon Chief would be the one to decide when and where the first fish were to be taken, and during the first few days of the run no one could eat Salmon; only the elders and children were allowed to eat and only if it were boiled. There would much prayer and singing. The ceremony could last five days before the Salmon could be taken from the river. The event occurred a couple of times during the year. The Salmon was our staple food and a small family had to get 3,000 pounds of dried fish to survive the winter months.

The men had a very important job and failure meant starvation for the People. Our territory was abundant and the elders could never remember a time in the past that the Salmon failed to come back to us.

The men hunted deer, elk, bear, moose, goat, sheep, antelope and caribou. These hunts were large and full of ceremony and great jubilation. The hunts for deer went something like this:

The men would gather their old moccasins and hang them on branches above a known deer trail, along both sides of the route. Then a corral would be built at the lower end of the trail at a point that would insure total capture. The young men would go out into the hills and forest and advance the deer herd toward the gorge. The deer would smell the old moccasins and be turned down the ravine toward the corral. When all of the deer reached the corrals, the gate was shut and the deer would be taken.

ANM Drawing

Goat and sheep hunts were along the Wenatchee, Chelan, Methow, and Similkameen territories back into the Cascade Range. The rest of the game animals were found everywhere in our traditional territory.

You should be told about some names, and how and what they are in Okanogan Country. Each of the names from Wenatchee, Washington to Salmon Arm, B.C., is for the most part names from our language, N'sylixcin. There are a few that will be obvious and some that I will tell you about. You will hear about the Wenatchee area first and then journey with me up the valley to the Northern end of our traditional territory at Enderby, B.C.

Names like Wenatchee, Entiat, Chelan, Methow, Okanogan, Tonasket, Osoyoos, Penticton, and Kelowna are names that have a definition and are an Okanogan Indian word.

Yet Omak is an Okanogan word that has no definition and it is simply a geographic location. Riverside, Oroville, Oliver, Summerland, Vernon are not of our language.

Names like Moses Lake named after Chief Moses, Nespelem after the area where an Okanogan Band lived like the San Poil, and Inchelium are place names.

Colville was the name of a man who had never stepped foot on the Colville Reservation, yet the reservation was named after him. Republic is obvious; Chesaw was named after a Chinese man married to an Okanogan Indian woman.

Did you know there is more than 50-plus spellings of the word "Okanogan"? Yes, and no one ever asked an Okanogan Indian. It all started with explorer David Thompson noting in his logbook that he could see ahead "the high woody mountains of the Cochenawga River". This first effort was what he thought the Indians were saying when they referred to the river and area known as "Okanogan".

Again, you should know about "Colville". There are no Colville Indians. It was a name given by President Grants' administration when the reservation was established. The Confederated Tribes of the Colville Reservation was named for a colonel named Colville. The man never set foot on the reservation.

The Southern end of our territory is Wenatchee, Washington. The Wenatchee People spoke Nxa amcxin some consider it a dialect of Nsyilxcn (Okanogan) language. Some of the words are a little different but one can converse easily amongst all of the Bands of the Okanogan People.

The Wenatchee People have the same custom, culture and tradition as all of the Bands of the Okanogan traditional territory. The children were raised and taught by the grandparents or the elders of the family. The children were taught from infancy as to their duties and things they must learn.

The girls were taught by the grandmother and had to learn all of the plants of the area, what they were, when they bloomed, what they were used for and at what quantity they were to be used.

They must learn to cook for two hundred as easily as for two, to care for the elderly and how to birth babies, care for the wounded, the sick, and sew, tan hides, build, take down and move Tule mat lodges, tipis, and pit houses; to know how to care for the children and where to go in time of crisis, raids, and epidemic. The girls had learned everything in their short youth, because there was no time for being a teenager.

The boys had to learn to hunt, fish, and protect the family. Their lot in life was hard and the lessons of life were long and arduous. The boys were taught by grandfather and you must learn to sing, drum, dance, and ceremonies. You had to learn to make weapons, learn how to fish, not for yourself, but for the village, for everyone. To hunt for many people and keep the children, elders and women constantly supplied with enough food. The duties seemed very hard for a boy to learn. But remember, they had no time to be kids, teenagers, to play all the time. They, like the girls, wanted to become men and women. To go with the men, to be respected like a man and ride with them to the hunting and fishing grounds, yes, and even to war. It was an honor to protect, defend and give your life for your People.

Boys didn't want to be treated like a boy. When they got to a certain age and noticed they were as big as some of the men and could do much of what they did. Then boys didn't want to stay in camp with the girls and do the bidding of the elders and take the orders of the grandmother all the time.

They wanted to ride with the men. The "quest" was a way to move toward manhood and the grandfathers would decide when this would happen.

The boys paid great attention to what grandfather said during that time. It was the dream of every boy to go with the men.

When the girls were reaching the age of womanhood and childbearing age and they were excited about going with the women. When they left the village and gathered roots, berries, and camped for weeks together and did whatever women did when they left the village. The girls too were excited about becoming a woman, as much as the boys wanting to be men.

I told you that we didn't have teenagers. Well, we didn't. They were an invention of Americas Industrial Revolution. At that time, kids were paid pennies a day and worked until they dropped, literally dropped dead. The sweat shops were a gift to the industrialist and a curse to the children. Then a law was passed to disallow the use of children in sweat shops. The industrialist then came up with a "teen" aged person that was not a child. So teenagers were invented to take the place of children. This practice lasted until just a short time ago, when laws developed and an age decided when teenagers could work legally.

The Okanogan Indian People had children that grew up to be men and women. That is why boys and girls worked so hard to learn the lessons and become young men and women.

The grandparents had the responsibility to teach all they knew of our custom, culture, religion, and tradition.

The way of our People was a good way and there was little strife among the Indians of the area. Our traditional enemies to the North were the Shu Shwap, to the East were the Blackfoot, and for a very short time the Yakima and Nez Perce to the South.

During the 1700's a war party from the South, made up predominately of Nez Perce and Yakima came to our country and were met at the Big Coulee by the Okanogan, San Poil, Nespelem warriors of the Okanogan Country. The battle lasted three days and two left on one horse. They never came back.

More than a hundred years had passed and our chiefs were offering protection to the great Chief Joseph of the Nez Perce, at Nespelem. Our People were not afraid of the government like other tribes of the West. We said we would protect him and his people so they would not be sent to their death in Florida. Chief Joseph is buried at the cemetery at Nespelem. There is much to say of Chief Joseph, and I think you will get much more from our local Tribal Language program, our library, and cultural museum in Coulee Dam.

If you look at our history you could not put a time to date the beginning. So I will begin with the influx of Europeans. It began at both ends of our traditional territories about 1805.

In the North, Fort Kamloops and the Hudson Bay Company and to the south when Lewis and Clark went to the mouth of the Columbia River.

The Brigade Trail from Ft. Kamloops to the soon to become Ft. Colville, David Thompson, and the development of Fort Okanogan at the mouth of the Okanogan River 1811, all contributed to the influx of trappers, then miners and finally settlers.

We are beginning our journey with the (Snpsqweusx) Wenatchee People. They spoke Nx amcxin, a dialect of Syilx language (Okanogan). The people far to the south, Kittitas, Yakama, Klickitat, and Walla Walla spoke Sahaptin and cannot be confused with being among our People.

Tule Mat Lodge ANM

The homes in the villages were either pit houses or Tule mat lodges. The pit house was about three to six feet into the ground and had logs across the top to a center that had a notched log for the exit of smoke and people.

The roof was covered with mats, hides, brush, grass and soil. It was about 30 feet in diameter and about 8 feet or more high at the center and the ones I saw had a burn pile at the southwest side of the house. We stopped using these pit houses early in the 1800's about the same time as the coming of the white man into our country.

The Tule mat lodge was about 16 feet high by about 60 feet long and had additional layers to repel water and wind. The floors were Tule mat and there would be two to eight families in such a lodge for the winter. The Tule mat lodge was quick to build and very sturdy to withstand the winters.

The summer had circular type Tule Mat lodge with a smoke screen on the top to regulate the smoke with the directions of the wind. Generally they used long poles to accomplish this and the entrance to the lodge was important, most often to the East.

Circular Tule Mat ANM

The other type was a community Tule mat lodge used for social obligations, seasonal trips, and fishing sites. They were the same size and on occasion larger than the Tule mat lodges I spoke of earlier. They were easily erected and removed and could be taken from place to place if need be. There was always enough Tule and lodge pole to build one anywhere.

The Wenatchee Bands lived near where the town now stands. Many of the Bands lived in the surrounding areas. The (villages) or towns were as follows:

The towns (villages) of the Wenatchee People were (to the South) at the mouth of Rock Island Creek, 7 miles South of Wenatchee at Stemilt Creek, opposite Moses Coulee near the mouth of Colocham creek, at the mouth of Squillchuck Creek, on the North side of Wenatchee River about one-half mile below Monitor, at Zena 8 miles North of the Wenatchee River,   at the mouth of Mission Creek, where Cashmere is located (the largest camp and most populated in winter), at the mouth of the Icicle Creek about a mile South of Leavenworth, at the site of present day Entiat, and just North of Vantage that was popular because it was unusually free of snow.

There are legends from the area and I have a couple you might like, they are of the "Two Sisters" south east of Wenatchee on Malaga Highway and of Saddle Rock behind Wenatchee. **"The Way I Heard It."**

The Owl Legend

In the early days owls used to eat people so when two owls saw a large encampment of Indians a short distance east of the mouth of Squillchuck Creek they were very happy. "Now we will have lots to eat" they said.

It happened that a little boy bird, which Indians called "Hat Hat", saw the owls approaching the camp. He knew they were up to no good. So, in order to save the people from the owls, he dived through each of their heads in turn, leaving large holes.

When this happened the owls and people were all turned to stone and this is why there were so many rocks and boulders along the Columbia for miles in that area.

On Saddle Mountain, just southeast of Wenatchee, a grizzly bear and another bear were fighting over their husband. Their children were playing near them. Then all of them were turned to stone, and if you look at the mountain you can still see them today; Grizzly Bear, the other Bear, the children, the owls, and the little boy "Hat Hat".

"The place of the "Rainbow Robe" Wenatchee (wa-nat-chee)

There are a number of legends defining the word "Wenatchee." The first white settlers came to the country they heard it called boiling waters meaning noisy water.

And another tale declaring it to be the name of mighty warrior who lived many, many years ago, when tradition was in it youth. He was called Chief Wenatchee, because he and his bands roamed this valley in undisputed derivation of the word.

By those who have made a comprehensive study of Indian traditions, it is said that Wenatchee is the title of one of the charm tales of the Indians, a chant told at pow wows.

It relates the story of an old love legend, and is derived from the tale of the Love Daughter of the

widowed Moon.   Beautiful
and possessed of all the graces
that contribute to make
maidens adorable, was the
young Princess. At first she
was admired and subsequently
passionately loved by the Sun.
But the Moon, according to
this legend, deemed the Sun much too old to woo
the fair Princess, not yet arrived at the age when
she knew her own heart, and had fixed her wish
upon the marriage of her daughter with a younger,

 if less dazzling, yet
handsome chief of
the sky.

But the wayward
maiden loved the
majestic Sun. For a
long period Mother
Moon remained
awake at night,
keeping vigil over the
movements of her
daughter, lest the mighty Sun should bear her
away. Already the Sun had woven for her a bridal
robe of threads spun from the rainbow, and one
day while the Moon slumbered the Princess

arrayed herself in this beautiful, luminous garment, and went down to the sea to wed with the Sun.

Shortly after her departure, the Moon awoke and hastened in pursuit of the fugitive lovers. On the bar of silvery lightning, hurled by her rejected lover from his place in the sky. In the dark despair of her terror the Princess flung her gorgeous mantle over the mountain top and concealed herself in the heart of the cliffs, where from that evil day until the present she has dwelt in seclusion, bewailing her sad fate.

It is the Indians' belief that her melancholy, yet musical voice floats out upon the wind whenever the night is still. The robe still hangs where it was cast by the frighted maiden, from the mountain top and over its sides, in the form of a river, and yet possessing all the hues of the rainbow, when the Sun comes down through gorge and glen to caress its rippling folds. And it is called Wa-Nat-Chee, or "Robe of the Rainbow."

The Wenatchee People had little to do with the white man in the beginning, but as time passed problems began to arise. By 1850 there were five separate bands of Wenatchee People who had been here since time began.

In 1855 Issac I. Stevens, Governor of Washington Territory and Superintendent of Indian Affairs were eager to complete the Northern Pacific Railroad across the territory. In order for Stevens to clear the way for the railroad and settlement, the Indian title to the land had to be eliminated. He called a treaty council of Indians of the region. Chief Tecolekun of the Wenatchee and Lahoom of the Entiat were there at the Yakima Treaty of 1855.

The treaty provided for the confederating of fourteen tribes into the Yakima Nation and the establishment of a large reservation in the Yakama Valley. And, to the Wenatchee Chief Tecolekun satisfaction, a six mile by six mile fishery reservation on the Wenatchee River. This treaty negotiation had several flaws. One was the lumping together of a great number of Indians that were culturally, geographically, and in language separate from the Wenatchee People. Governor Stevens expected all tribes to relocate to Yakama. The Wenatchee had no desire to move from their traditional lands and homes. The government was to survey the "Fishery Reservation" that did not happen.

The next year under the command of Colonel Wright, all Indians were to accept the reservation status.

Near the town of Leavenworth, Wright met the Wenatchee Chief Skamow, who negotiated to stay in their valley. Even though the "Fishery Reservation," treaty was signed by the two leaders, a survey still was not done.

The years following that treaty were bloody ones and by 1858 peace was declared east of the Cascade Mountains. After the Civil War many of our Chiefs went to Washington D.C. to try to get a 'fair shake' with the government. By 1884 many of the Indians had made the journey to the Yakama and Colville Reservation.

But since the Wenatchee had a "Fishery Reservation" they refused to relocate. In 1884 some of the Wenatchee's filed claims under the Indian Homestead Act. And no survey was completed on the fishery reservation yet.

By 1888 George W. Gordon, Office of Indian Affairs Agent, was sent by the government to evaluate the Fishery Reservation problem. Gordon had no interpreter and depended completely on facts given to him by the local white people. In the Treaty of 1855, the reservation as defined by "forks in the Wenatchee River," but which forks? Gordon chose to pick out the forks which best suited the whites further up in the mountains where the lands were comparatively worthless, being composed of rugged mountains, rifted with deep canyons. And still no survey was conducted.

In the fall of 1892, Agent Jay Lynch, headquartered in Yakama, was directed to resolve the problem and to definitively locate the reservation. Lynch ventured to the now booming Wenatchee River Valley did not find it politically expedient to concur with the Indians belief that the reservation was to be centered upon the great ancestral fishery at the mouth of the Icicle River at Leavenworth. He recommended that the reservation be surveyed in the rugged terrain between Lake Wenatchee and the Chi Wawa.

In 1893 forty-one white settlers petitioned the President demanding that the Indian Treaty Rights be sold. Almost immediately the Indian Agents at Yakama received instructions to commence negotiations with the Yakama Nation to obtain a cession of Indian Rights to the Fishery Reservation.

The Yakima's were to be offered $10,000 for giving up their claims to the reservation. The negotiations would be transacted with the council of fourteen member tribes, all of which were Sahaptin speaking people with no close ties to the Wenatchee Indians, even language. The Wenatchee Tribe was deliberately deprived of representation. In the dead of winter 1893 Chief John Harmelt argued for the Wenatchee People. He refused to accept the proposed reservation and refused to accept money for the land because it didn't belong to him. He insisted that the land promised the Wenatchee's in 1856 by Colonel Wright was the land between the Icicle and Peshastin Creeks.

Agent Irwin countered the Wenatchee's and said they could acquire title to their ancestral homelands through the land allotment program, that they didn't need the fishery reservation to own their land. When the council voted on the issue, the decision to cede the rights passed 67 to 25. Chief Harmelt returned to confer with his People.

After two weeks another council was convened without the Wenatchee Chiefs and the Yakama leaders offered to relinquish their rights for $20,000. On August 15, 1894 Congress ratified the bill abrogating all Indian claims to the historic fishery. Two hundred and forty-six Indians signed the agreement; but not one Wenatchee. The $20,000 was promptly invested by the Yakama's in an irrigation project for the Yakima Valley.

The Wenatchee People had been promised that special land allotting agents would be sent to arrange for acquiring land near the growing community called Mission. Agent Irwin did arrive to offer the tribes $9 per person to surrender their land rights. The Wenatchee's refused and all the remaining land was swiftly claimed by the arriving white settlers.In 1898 Chief Harmelt and Louis Judge took their cause to Washington D.C. The white community countered that action with a petition of their own and the issue of the Fishery Reservation was killed again. In February 1900, Chief Harmelt tried again to seek appropriation for assist and improve the lands they did possess.

Again this attempt failed. By 1904 the town of Mission became Cashmere and the government provided $155 to each of the thirty Indian families remaining in the valley to use for agricultural supplies and implements for the domestic needs of their People.

Chief Harmelt and family ANM

Chief Harmelt tried one last time to receive compensation for the illegal sale of their reservation. The claim was rejected. By 1927 only four Indian families remained in Cashmere. During the 1930s Chief Harmelt continued to speak for just compensation and justice for his People. On July 3, 1937 Chief Harmelt and his wife died in a fire at their home up the Nahahum Canyon.

There still has been no survey of the "Fishery Reservation."

There is more to this story and most of it is documented somewhere in your local library. I invite you see how it ended.

Chief Harmelt and the other chiefs of the Wenatchee over the period of middle 1800s and the early 1900s remembered many tragedies but on the White River was the only massacre. This is an account of the massacre.

"The day was horrible when the soldiers surrounded the encampment and ordered the males to line up and be shot down totally. Some were hung, and to complete the decimation women and children were then shot or slashed to death with sabers."

This description written by Moses George helps to recall one of the uglier incidents out of early Wenatchee area history. He told this story at a Chamber luncheon in Wenatchee some years ago.

The increasing incidents between Indians and miners in the 1850's, led to army forts throughout the Washington territory and expeditions to apprehend and punish Indians guilty of murdering miners. The White River Massacre started something like this:

"In 1858 Col. George Wright took one expeditionary force to Walla Walla and Maj. Robert Garnett led the second group from Fort Simcoe some 30 miles west of Yakama then north. Maj. Garnett left the fort with

306 men and 225 horses on August 10, 1858.

Three days later they were in the Kittitas valley where Yakama Indian guides led troops with Lt. Jesse Allen into the country along Swauk Creek and Teanaway River. Lt. Allen was accidently shot in the back by one of his men, but the expedition continued. The troops captured a village on the Teanaway River and the Yakama guides pointed out five Indians they deemed guilty of a murder of some miners and they were tied up and shot.

The rest of the troop found Indians along the Icicle and near Leavenworth and killed another five Indians pointed out by Yakama Indian guides as looking like the murderers. The troops then regrouped where Wenatchee now stands. The Yakima Indian guides claimed another ten murderers were at Lake Wenatchee, so Lt. Garnett sent 60 troops back up the Wenatchee River.

The troops went to where the Wenatchee Indians gathered each fall. When they arrived they found no Indians. The troop split up and half crossed the Chiwawa and made contact with a party of Indians at

Raging Creek.   The only evidence of any killings was some unidentified graves found there later.

The second group went up the White River where they found 10 teepees and about 70 Wenatchee's five miles up the river from Lake Wenatchee.   They had no idea of the miners killed or the reason for the soldiers advancing at such a speed.   When a few went out to see what was the matter the firing began and it didn't take long before all of the Indians in camp were dead.

Only a few boys tending horses a short distance from the camp survived the massacre. They heard the shots and screams of the slaughter and left after the soldiers left.

Turtle Rock   ANM

The journey north up the Columbia River takes you around Turtle Rock. There may be stories about this rock, but I could find no credible ones at the Wenatchee Valley Museum and Cultural Center, Tribal Historical Department, and the library.

The Columbia River, before river dams, did not pass on both sides of the rock.

The name seems to be a local (non) Indian story.

Next stop is Entiat, and as you go by you must know that the original town is below the water line just below the town of Entiat. You can still see it just below the waterline at the park. This is **"The Way I Heard It"**:

"During the building of the original bridge, an old Indian Woman and young girl were questioning the Engineer putting in the abutments to the bridge on the North side next to the town.

The old woman was trying to convince the Engineer that to disturb the grave yard would be very bad. The Engineer listened and argued for a time and after a few days of this simply told the old woman that the bridge was going in and there was nothing she could do; they would relocate what bones they found but would not stop the bridge from going in on time.

The old woman was furious and warned the Engineer that a terrible thing would happen to everyone here. The Engineer was polite but steadfast and asked only what she was talking about. The old woman said, "If you build this bridge and disturb this ancient grave site, that before this little girl is grown, everything will be under water!" This was taken as a pretty good laugh and dismissed quickly.

The little girl told me the story when she was an elder and said she had almost forgotten about it. But, when she heard that the town of Entiat would be moved and that the highway and railroad line would be inundated by the water; she remembered the story.

The lady has passed away but her story will never be forgotten; now you will keep it alive, for her."

The next place you will come to is the Bee Bee Bridge below Chelan Falls. The ancient story is that the glacier that covered North America stopped at the Bee Bee Bridge and receded from there about 11 thousand years ago.

The stories of the area are many and colorful. Some of the stories were of how the Indians dealt with the influx of people into this area. In 1875 the Okanogan, Methow, Chelan and Entiat Bands drove the Chinese out of the area. They attacked the Chinese miners at the mouth of the Methow River and a few miles south of Chelan Falls killing about 300 Chinese miners. The other Chinese living in the area deserted the village across the river from Chelan Falls about the same time.

After that Chinese population remained small and was seen ferrying people across the Columbia River. By 1895 only one Chinese miner was left and if not for the kindness of a local miner named James Mather's, he would have died.

The Chinese miner fell ill and had a claim across from Mather's. Mather's recognized there was no smoke from the cabin and noticed the mule was not moved to better pasture. Mather's crossed over and found the Chinese miner, Que Yu sick with the fever. Mather's boiled water and wrapped Que Yu in wool blankets and soaked him in hot water until the fever went down.   He made a prairies hen soup and moved Que Yu to their camp.

Que Yu got well and helped the Mather's by improving their rocker in their slues which were poorly done.   Que Yu showed them how to improve it and Mather's, who had previously earned $1.00 over sixty days of work, made a phenomenal amount after the improvements.

Pateros   ANM

As you travel past Wells Dam you will be coming onto a place called Pateros at the mouth of the Methow River. The Okanogan's lived there in three small villages. One up the Methow a mile or two, one at the mouth and one down the Columbia River a mile or two. Each had a few hundred people and one was the winter home of the People that lived there.

This story was told to me by my mother and she said it was at a spot near the town of Pateros, up the Methow River a ways. She was told the story when she was very young and she remembered it because of the taking of a young man.

She said they (the Sasquatch) seldom took young girls but always keep aware that you are being watched when you are out in the wilderness. There is always a strong scent and you will know when they are near you, and this was rare. They will let you know they are near only if they want you to know. This is **"The Yay I Heard it"**:

A family that consisted of a very young girl child, a boy about 9 years old, a teenage girl, a boy of about 16 or 17 years, and a young man with a wife and child. They all lived together with the parents. Each year the family would go to a place on the river that was green and lush and quiet. Each year the family would be together without the rest of the people of the village around, just the family.

The years had gone by quietly and the family grew strong and proud. The place on the River had plenty of hunting and fishing spots to keep the family fed and the kids happy.

One day the older boys went up the river to be together and just have some fun. They played games with the younger brothers and tried some fishing. The middle boy, the one about 16 years old, went off from the rest for awhile. The boys seemed not to worry; he often left for no reason and always came back.

The time was getting late and they began to worry, they hollered and searched for him, but in vein. They went back to their parents and told them the boy did not return and they did not know what to do. The father gathered relatives and went to find his son. The search lasted for days and no sign of the boy. The grief of the mother and children was inconsolable, and the family went back to the village.

Sasquatch ANM

18 foot tall metal sculpture by Smoker Marchand.
Located on Disautel Pass, WA.

Each year, the family went back to the summer camp and searched and waited for the boy. The oldest son was now the eldest in the family; the father had passed away, never knowing the whereabouts of his son. The eldest kept the custom going, and always returned to the summer camp year after year. Then one day the eldest son was sitting by the river and he heard something across the river making noise. He waited and from the brush, came a man in animal skins and he looked familiar! The eldest stood up and called to the man and the man answered in broken language, but it was Okanagan Indian.

They talked and the now eldest found his brother that had been taken by the Sasquatch that summer morning so long ago. The eldest said to come home and see the family, and how everyone had grown and mother was still alive and always spoke of him. That it would be a time of celebration!

The man said sadly that he could not go with his brother. That he had a family of his own and children.

That he was allowed to see his brother and tell the family not to come here anymore, and that he would not be back ever again.

The man said he was allowed to come this one time; and that he did see the family each year they came to this place. In the beginning he was sad. But as the years passed he found comfort in his new family and became committed and could not leave.

The two waved and said "good bye" (a word that does not exist in the Okanogan language. It is a way to speak to someone you will never see again, as at a funeral, you say good bye). The two parted and the family never returned to the site again.

Fort Okanogan Sign   ANM

One story of Fort Okanogan that will be dismissed by some local historians and writers has been told and this is **"The Way I Heard It"**:

After Ft. Okanogan was first built the local Okanogan Indians were less than happy about the new neighbors.

The place was attacked and to say it was destroyed is kind of a joke. The first "fort" was made of drift wood and scraps and did little to protect the inhabitants from anything. The news of this incident arrived and the headquarters in Victoria had already sent one Alexander Ross. He commanded a post at Vancouver and was ordered to punish the locals and rebuild the post.

Ross was well equipped and had with his a party of voyageurs and flotilla bateaux carrying a few brass 4 pounders and started up the Columbia River. After a weary portage through the Dalles and up the Columbia to what is now Rock Island, where the Northern R&R crosses the Columbia River they had their first encounter. The Wenatchee Indians had a short encounter and withdrew. They portaged around the rapids and began the last stage of the journey.

The Okanogan Indians made great preparations to drive the invaders back and protect their land. They had an armada of canoes and members of many of the Okanogan Band, Methow, Chelan, Nespelem and San Poil prepared to engage the enemy. They would wait in the concealed spot just back from the mouth of the Okanogan River and then annihilate the surprised enemy. Because Ross had encountered Indians in his journey he was cautious of any arrival of his group on new shores. Ross arrived opposite the mouth of the Okanogan River and the engagement began. The Indians used arrows to pour down on the enemy from their place of hiding. This was answered with musket fire and then the use of the 4 pounders turned the tide of battle.

Eager to inflict much merited punishment on the Indians who were thus, providentially, placed almost within their grasp, the Hudson Bay Men pursued the fleeing Indians who, now anxious for nothing but to escape, made what haste they could to reach the foothills and safety. The whites with their artillery and musketry shot down all who could be reached and without mercy. Ross, in his report of the occurrence, says with the brevity of our own People: "I met the Indians at the Okanogan and buried 118 on the spot where they fell. Those who were not buried floated down the river."

Discovered while working on the grade at Swansea recently a much rusted sphere of iron, which is undoubtedly one of the cannon balls fired at the Indians, is in the possession of local person. That person has presented it to the state historical society as proof of the attack and received no response. But such is life in the wilderness; the only believable proof must be made by someone other than a local white person and never an Indian.

Ft. Okanogan, a site near Highway 97 junctions with SR #17 near the mouth of the Okanogan River is now owned and operated by the Colville Tribes.

Stanley Drawing of Fort Okanogan
1855

Okanogan Natives seen in front of the 2nd
location of Fort Okanogan, Oregon (now
Okanogan County, Washington State)

Heritage Productions

We are now moving along #97, north along the Okanogan River toward Monse. There is a village site near here and it was a permanent home for The Okanogans and these Indians were the first to meet both David Thompson and later Alexander Ross when the fort was being built. There is a Salmon fishing site just up the river from here, but a great deal of their fishing was done at the mouth of the river.

There were still gatherings during the early part of the last century just near the mouth of the river. There were horse racing, gambling, trading and a lot of fishing

Chiliwist Jim and family   ochs

When the Grand Coulee Dam went in a lot of things changed among our People and along the river.

You should have passed through the sandy bench and onto a stretch of highway going toward Malott.

This was an area that another Indian village (town) was near. West across the river, is the road up to the Chiliwist country. One of our last Indian Medicine Men and highly respected man was called Chiliwist Jim came from that country. Two of his grandsons were Norris Palmanteer and Eddie Palmanteer, both were Tribal leaders and well respected among our People and throughout Indian Country.

There are pictures of Chiliwist Jim found in some books at the Okanogan County Historical Society in Okanogan. And it is a good place to investigate some of your interests in our country.

As you proceed toward Okanogan, a town named after our people, it is odd that there is no mention of that in the history of the town.

If you go into Okanogan and turn left on highway #20 you will be near the Sheep Slaughter Site. It's on the westside of the river and can be visited by turning into Okanogan and staying on highway #20 going toward Twisp/Winthop. It will be a few miles outside of Okanogan, and there will be a sign showing you the site.

This was cattle country, too, and the winter of 1889-1890 was the "Cow Killing Winter". In 1889, about 120 years ago, the towns of Ruby and Loop Loop were booming as Washington became a state of the Union. During the year, the county suffered from dry weather and unbelievable swarms of crickets and yellow jackets. The fall saw normal rains and December brought a foot of snow to cover the county.

It was recorded by pioneers throughout the county that a snow storm began on the first day of 1890 with a powder snow being blown in from the north. The temperature dropped to -25 degrees in Ruby.

The blizzard lasted two weeks and left cold temperatures and large snow drifts in its wake.

"(Its) the worst storm of the season and claimed by old timers to be the worst in 40 years," stated the Wilbur Register in 1890.

The livestock were found huddled in ravines and stumbling in drifts of snow so they could not escape. Hundreds of livestock died from the storm and its effects left behind, after it passed. That's where the term "cow killing winter" came from.

It was recorded that Thomas Roberts, a Welsh immigrant, drove nine of his milk cows and some calves from Conconully towards, what is now Omak, to take them to a lower elevation near the Okanogan River.

Roberts broke trail for his livestock using snowshoes and reached his goal at about 9 pm the next day. He warmed himself in Uriah Ward's cabin and the next morning the men set out to find several of the cattle frozen to death, standing upright, with hay before them. One of the cows that died was found standing next to two calves that shared her fate.

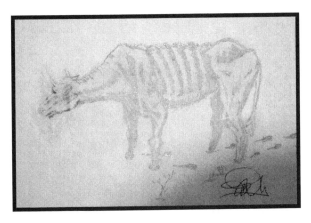

Starving cow by Arnie Marchand

When the snow began to melt, the pioneers believed that relief was in sight but once the freezing cold returned more livestock died. The ground, wet from the melting snow, had frozen to form a crust that was impenetrable by the cattle and the horses towards the beginning of February 1890.

A combination of the seasons' weather conditions had already left hay in short supply and pioneers had to find different ways to sustain their livestock.

Dr. J.I. Pogue, who lived on the flat above Omak that bears his name, was recorded as turning to feeding salted meat from animals that had died, in an attempt to save his prized herd of 150 well bred horses. With the meat, Pogue fed them a mixture of boiled potatoes, bran, and flour. This saved roughly a third of his horses.

It was said that Chief Tonasket, Chief Sarsarpkin, and a few other ranchers farther north had put up hay and saved almost half of their cattle that winter.

Some pioneers turned to feeding their horses and livestock anything from willow brush, straw from beds, grain intended for crops to biscuits baked strictly for feeding cows. Throughout the county livestock losses were devastating. The counties property tax base was based mainly on livestock and many families only wealth were the horses and cattle that perished. Out of a hundred head of beef cattle which were turned into a cottonwood grove in hopes of them surviving, only one 4 year old steer survived.

Virginia Grainger noted that there were no real numbers of lost livestock by the estimated that 10,000 animals or 90% of the horses and cattle were lost during that winter.

John Thompson had 1,200 cattle and roughly a hundred tons of hay when the "cow killing" winter started, but was left with only 96 when it was over.

On the Chiliwist Creek, the L.C. Malott family and W.L. Davis family and the Hedges Brothers entered the cattle business in 1889 and brought 200 cattle into the county. During the winter they lost all but a few. The Malotts had the one steer, out of 200, that survived the winter. They had been financed by a friend from Seattle and it was recorded that it took him 20 years and the sale of his ranch in 1909 to pay off the debt caused by the winter. That storm not only killed livestock, but cut off communication with the rest of the newly formed state.

Trains that ran to and through the county were shut down as the rails were impassible from snow drifts. Over a thousand pounds of mail piled up as the railroad was unable to come north past Wilbur. The Okanogan River was useless to ferries as the river had over two feet of ice covering it as well as a foot of snow. The booming towns of Ruby and Conconully were snowed in for seven weeks. The winter didn't last forever but the people who lived during that time must have felt like it had.

If you cross into Okanogan you will see the signs to Salmon Creek road and you will find the marker for where the city of Ruby was and the way to get to Conconully. It is a very nice drive and a pleasant side trip.

If you don't visit the site continue traveling between Okanogan and Omak. Omak is an Okanogan Indian word that has no meaning; it is considered a "place name" and has no definition. There were a few who said "omache" meant something or other, but when the Tribes put out their first Okanogan Language Dictionary, Omak had no definition.

Near the Okanogan County Fair Grounds, on your right, as you travel north, is another permanent place where we lived. As you come into the Omak area there are many stories from here. But, first you must know that no one lived in the area of Omak. Our main village was four miles north along the river near the CIPP mill site. That area was the place where a village of some two to four hundred peoples lived in permanent residence.

City of Omak

Omak had a few distinctions, one that it was the only place where a green reed grew in the entire traditional area. The green reed grew in the swamp area about where the football field is and it was about six feet high and had a white flower that bent down along a stout stem and a few wide long green leaves. An elder named Ms. Isabel Arcasa told me that story and she was well into her late 90's.

Another interesting aspect is that on the small hill above the swamp, about where the high school is today, Indian grave sites were disturbed during the building of a toll bridge in Omak. The rocks over the graves were used for the bridge piers, even though the local Indians didn't like it, they were moved anyway. The bridge washed out a short time later by a river jam.

I didn't say this to make it sound so bad, only that the towns' father Ben Ross got here in 1901 and the building came after that. Ben Ross is called the "father" of Omak and was an energetic family man who was the initial promoter in organizing a school district. He is responsible for the plating of Omak in 1907.

St. Mary's Mission is East up the hill from Omak and Omak Lake is near the mission. The mission was the first site settled in the area in 1886 by a priest named Father De Rouge. The mission became a junior college with dormitories and a boarding school for our People.

St. Mary's Mission   ANM

The land was given to the Church by Chief Smitkin who was a devout and generous man. His families are still in the area and take great pride in their ancestry.

St. Mary's Mission was destroyed and rebuilt four times by 1919. It has remained a boarding school until the middle of the last century. In 2005 the new Pascal Sherman Indian School was built adjacent the original St. Mary's Mission site. It is a truly beautiful and wondrous site to see. There are many people on the Reservation that remember very clearly the boarding school days at St. Mary's Mission.

The Okanogan County Heritage magazine published this in their quarterly newsletter, the Okanogan County Heritage, fall 1988. The title was:

"Okanogan County's First College"
by David Lindeblad

David Lindeblad was a native of Spokane, and attended Eastern Washington University where he received a master's degree in the history and philosophy of education. He has been a past vice president of the county historical museum committee, and at this time he had been a teacher and the Associate Dean for Wenatchee Valley-North Community College and later Dean of the college.

With permission of the author it is reprinted here.

It was the work of one man, the indefatigable Fr. Etienne deRouge, who developed a curricula outstanding for its time.

The story of Jesuit missionary Etienne deRouge and his establishment of St. Mary's mission are well known. What has been largely forgotten is how Father deRouge began the first college in Okanagan County.

St. Mary's was founded near Ellisforde in 1885. Early that spring Father deRouge built a small log cabin near the Okanogan River, and it was from that site he began his missionary work among the Okanogan Indians. It was there, too, that Okanogan County's first actual "school" was begun. Classes were held on a regular basis, and a basic curriculum established.

DeRouge was member of the Society of Jesus, commonly known as the Jesuits, founded in the sixteenth century by a charismatic Basque priest, Ignatius of Loyola. Jesuit priest soon became the Catholic Church's special emissaries to indigenous people throughout the world.

In 1885, deRouge moved his budding mission to a more centralized location near Omak Lake.

DeRouge was in the midst of a difficult situation as the United States endeavored to treat the Indians by placing them on reservations and transforming them into an agricultural people. But conflict was inevitable. DeRouge realized quite fully that Indians must be allowed to retain a portion of their lands and culture and that education would be the key element in a successful policy.

During the initial growth years of Okanogan County, when the first silver mines were opened and the first cattlemen settled permanently in the valley, and shortly before the regions fruit industry began to take hold, St. Mary's mission grew and prospered.

From the beginning, deRouge strove for quality. He recruited the best teaching staff available. Trained teachers came from all over the world to teach at St. Mary's. DeRouge appealed to Catholic groups to send their best, and in many cases they did just that. Quality and innovation were the watchwords.

St. Mary's Mission school was first in many aspects of the history of education in Okanogan County. The first use of typewriters in class, the first foreign language curriculum, the first music classes as a requirement for graduation, and the longest average school year for any county school before World War I, and many, many other first all are indications of quality. Many non-Indian children also attended the mission school. Their parents no doubt were attracted by one of the most advanced curricula in the state.

By 1910 Father deRouge even had the rudiments of a basic college curriculum in place. Classes were taught by scholastics, brothers, and even by deRouge himself. Latin, Greek, calculus, Early and modern History and college level mathematics all were available to the more advanced more motivated students. These were the first college level courses offered in Okanogan County.

Classes were not offered in the strict sense of a semester or a quarter. Rather, students who showed aptitude were encouraged to take advantage of advanced instruction. In 1924, one of the more illustrious early graduates of St. Mary's mission, Paschal Sherman, moved directly into junior class at St. Martins' College at Lacey. He had no trouble in the transition.

These were the days, too, when a college education meant a different curriculum than it does today. Most American colleges at the turn of the century stressed a classical European tradition. Subjects such as philosophy, math, foreign language, history and English were the core of a college education. Vocational or commercial courses were virtually non-existent.

When Sherman moved on to the Catholic University in Washington D.C., where he attended graduate school, he had been sufficiently prepared at St. Mary's to pass qualifying exams in French and German.

DeRouge followed a pattern as he developed his mission. He would slowly implement changes in his programs and curriculum until that day when those changes had sufficiently evolved to become a permanent part of St. Mary's. What a tragedy it was for the entire community, then, when fate interceded and the Okanogan's first college was dealt two blows from which it would never recover.

The first came in the early evening on May 11, 1916, when deRouge, at the age of 56 died. His death was sudden and surprise a to the entire community. He had worked tirelessly to see his mission become the finest educational institution in North Central Washington. But like many charismatic leaders, he made no provision for his work to be carried on by like – minded individuals. His successors concentrated on saving what had already been gained, and further growth was stunted.

The second blow came on October 5, 1919, when the college burned to the ground. The building that houses the college also served as a dormitory, and mission's distractive headquarters, the museum, and the library.

Although of suspicious nature, the cause of the fire was never determined. What is known is that it was first discovered on the third floor in an unused garret. By the time alarms had sounded, the building was ablaze. Vandals had placed some large rocks in the water tank pipes for the mission's water system, and there was insufficient water pressure to fight the fire.

This was a wooden frame building over 12,000 square feet. There were three towers, one on each end and one in the middle. The fire swept quickly through the structure, which was reduced to ashes.

The loss was great. The boys' dormitory was gone, the museum was gone, most of the band instruments were gone, and Father deRouge's personal correspondence all went up in flames, lost too, were several paintings by deRouge.

The library, largest of its kind in the region, had contained over 2,000 volumes. The museum, a potpourri of stuffed animals, birds, artifacts, and rock samples was a *particularly galling loss. It represented hundreds of hours of effort by numerous students and teachers. This marked the close of the early golden age of St. Mary's mission. Okanogan County was put on hold for the next 50 years until Wenatchee Valley Community College would begin to develop its northern curriculum and campus.*

Balancing Rock at Omak Lake ANM

There is a "Balancing Rock" near Omak Lake that weighs 30 to 40 tons and is balanced on a stone the size of your fist. It is a site to see and is a short quarter mile hike off the road. A site you should see and send the picture to friends.

If you look to the East up the wide valley toward Disautel you are looking at a story that happened there in the early part of the last century. A friend of mine told me this story. He was reluctant to tell it, but I am the godfather of his son Nick, so I can tell you, this is **"The Way I Heard It"**:

A little girl was living with her grandmother in a small cabin a few miles out of Omak. One day in the late summer a man came riding up and the little girl ran to her grandmother in fear. The man had steely eyes and did not speak.

The old woman went out to meet the man and they talked a short time and then he rode off. The old woman told the girl to get wood for the fire and they would start dinner. The little girl did as she was told and wondered why they were cooking so soon in the day? The old woman was afraid of the man but showed no outward signs of that fear to the little girl. The man came back after an hour and ate, said something to the old woman and left.

The little girl watched the man disappear into the forest going east toward Nespelem. She asked her grandmother what they talked about and who was the man?

She said his name was Johnny McClain and he had just robbed a bank and was to hide the gold near them and that he would return to get it. She said he thanked her for the food and left.

Sometime later news came to the cabin by way of the local law man. He said that Johnny McClain wanted to talk to the old woman and that he would take them to Walla Walla prison to meet with him. The old woman was afraid again, and said she was in fear of that man and would not go speak to him. The law man tried to convince the old woman but to no avail.

So, as you look up that small valley toward Nespelem you can imagine the gold still there but where?

Yes, Johnny McClain did rob a bank up North and was a know bank robber and gunman. And yes, he did hide the money and often returned to the area to get money and leave to do his business.

And no, one to this day knows where the gold was hid, because the old woman died a few years after that and the little girl that told the story told her son and he said his mom died when he was a little boy, but he remembered the story. The gold is still there resting comfortably.

Traveling to Conconully   ANM

North and west of Omak there is a town called Conconully nestled back in the hills. It was named after an Okanogan Chief named ConconNulx and his people lived there in a permanent village (town). It was the county seat after the town of Ruby had it and then it moved to Okanogan. We have a great history, however short, in this area.

One of those stories was the shootout at a local bar. This was given to me by the Okanogan County Sheriff, Frank Rogers. The story is titled: **"Shootout at the Lute Morris Saloon"** and **"The Way I Heard It":**

Sorely troubled, Alfred Allsworth (Fred) Thorp, Sheriff of Okanogan County approached the Lute Morris Saloon in Conconully Monday morning, November 9, 1909. Inside, a hard-looking stranger of medium height, with black hair and a mustache, who gave his name as Frank LeRoy, was playing cards at a table.

Sheriff Thorp intended to question LeRoy regarding a safe blown in the A.C. Gillespie & Son store in Brewster a few days earlier and two residential burglaries in Brewster.

A mild mannered Iowa farmer, Thorp came to the Okanogan in 1900, carried mail between Chesaw and Loomis, ran for sheriff. Armed with a six-shooter, Thorp feared only that some day, he might have to kill someone, which would compel him to resign, and this might be the day.

LeRoy sat very still, watching the frontier sheriff approach the card table. "I'll have to take you in, partner." said Thorp. There must have been an unearthly silence in the saloon as LeRoy rose. Thorp drew his revolver, "I'm going to search you." LeRoy turned as if to throw off his coat, and then jerked a pistol from a shoulder holster.

The two opened fire simultaneously LeRoy dancing about to present an elusive target. LeRoy got off four shots. Thorp emptied his revolver, striking LeRoy's right hand, causing him to drop his gun, and hitting the suspect in the shoulder as he bolted out a rear door.

LeRoy staggered a few yards up Salmon Creek before hiding in some brush. "Look out, he's got another gun" someone yelled from across the creek. Having borrowed a second revolver, the sheriff pounced, kicking LeRoy's gun from his hand.

LeRoy was rolled onto a piece of barn board and carried into the Elliot Hotel. There his wounds, including a punctured lung were treated. In LeRoy's hotel room Thorp found two more guns, wedges and drills, and a supply of nitroglycerine.

Two days later, LeRoy broke out of the county jail. Wearing only his nightshirt, a blanket for trousers, shoes and an old mackinaw taken from an elderly trusty who served as jailer, the desperado flew through chilling weather to Okanogan. Three days later, Thorp caught up with him in a field of sagebrush below Malott. LeRoy came out with his hands up commenting mildly he wished he had a gun so the two could shoot it out again.

In January, 1910, at Conconully LeRoy was convicted of burglarizing the William Plemmon's home at Brewster. Since this was his third burglary conviction, he was sentenced to life imprisonment in the state penitentiary at Walla Walla as a habitual criminal.

After serving nine years, LeRoy, in ill health, was released in 1919. He once met Fred Thorp on a street in Spokane. They chatted for a few minutes. While there were, in pioneer times, numerous other confrontations between armed men, the Thorp-LeRoy gun fight probably was the closest Okanogan County ever came to a <u>HIGH NOON</u> shootout.

To the southeast is a place called Kartar Valley, east of Omak Lake. Ms Marie Picard George told this story of her father-in-law, Koxit George in 1973. Koxit George was born near the Entiat River; his name was La 'Homt. This is: **"The Way I Heard It"**:

The ten year old Indian boy rode his pinto mustang slowly into the murky shadows of the first greasewood bushes in the foothills of the mountains north of Omak Lake. Here, for the first time he dared to turn and search the trail behind him. He stared at the brown grassy slopes until his eyes ached. The boy could not detect a sign of movement, but the serenity of the terrain did not allay his fears.

As the he kicked his pony into a jog up the twisting, treacherous trail toward home in Kartar Valley, he remembered his father's final words of caution. "Son," he said "we are being watched, so we have to be careful. You must do exactly as I say."

The child recalled how proud he was when his father asked him to translate his business requests to the banker in Okanogan. When his father handed the banker his savings book, the boy said they wished to withdraw $2500 in greenbacks and $2500 in gold coin.

"Aren't you afraid someone will rob you, George?" teased the banker. "That is a lot of cash to carry around.'

"I need it to pay off my cowboys and to buy previsions for winter." After stuffing the money into the pockets of his big coat, the man and his son walked to the livery stable down by the river. While saddling their horses, his father had stuffed the paper money into the boy's yellow angora chaps and he used to large safety pins to secure the greenbacks in the pockets. Then he carefully placed the small sacks of $20 gold pieces in the saddle bags of the pinto pony.

"I need you to help me. So today you must forget your childish thoughts and games and act as a man" his father had warned him their native tongue. "Because of this money we are in great danger. There are thieves watching us who intend to rob us."

"Son, mount your pony and ride to Omak. Tie your horse at Jake Fink's Harness and Saddle Shop. Go into his store and shop around as you usually do. But watch your horse and if anyone acts interested in the saddle bags or horse, tell Mr. Fink right away."

"Before long I will arrive. I will not speak to you; don't speak to me. After I go into the store, you will get on your horse and ride slowly out of town. Take the trail toward home. You will not look back until you reach the trees and high hills of Markain Pass. Then you hide there and watch the back trail for me. If I appear in the valley below and men are riding with me, then you must steal through the brush and trees until you are out of sight. When you are safe from view whip your horse and ride for home as fast as possible. Give the money to your mother when you arrive home; she will know what to do with it. If I am alone, then wait for me."

The small boy waited, hidden in the bushes. Fear chewed his stomach like a starved wild animal. At last he heard the rhythmic cadence of a galloping horse. Soon his father appeared over the rise, alone, and riding relaxed and easy in a slow gallop. The boy and the man rode home together.

The above narrative sounds like a typical fictional old west story. But it is only one true account of many such incidents in the life of Koxit George, wealthy cattleman, benefactor of his people and patron of St. Mary's Mission. The boy was his son, Moses George, who lived near his father's old home ranch in Kartar Valley. His grandson is Wendell George the author of the book "Coyote Stories;" you should read it.

Another story told to me by a lady, an elder, who loved to talk about the times in early Omak. This is: **"The Way I Heard It"**;

She said some of the houses build by the river in East Omak were on stilts and a foot ramp was used to get to the house. Usually a tent was used to house some of the family in the back of the house.

One late afternoon two men showed up at the house of the old woman and the children were very afraid. One of the men had eyes that more than stared into you and seemed not to blink. The other man was a loud, seemingly happy and mostly intoxicated. The two had a beautiful young woman with them.

The old woman sent all of the children out of the house and into the tent while she stayed to fix dinner for the guests. They were loud and laughter was often. The old woman returned to the tent.

The night came early and the conversations became even louder in the house. Then an argument ensued. The one man roared his disapproval of the other man taking the woman anywhere. The words turned to violence. Then there was silence. A shot rang out. The children were terrified and were sure the men would come to kill or molest them. They huddled in the tent in fear. Then the old woman said the men were leaving and to keep quiet until they left.

The night grew into a long fearful silence and some of the children finally slept. The morning sun was above Omak Mountain when the old woman decided to leave the tent and go see what had happened in the house.

She came back and told one of the older boys to go get the constable. The boy returned and said he wouldn't come right away because he had other duties. The old woman went to the house and a few neighbors came to help.

The two men arguing over the beautiful young woman were a John McClain, outlaw and killer, and a local man whose first name was ......, well I cannot tell you.

You see his family is still living in East Omak and know nothing of this story about their Grandfather or Great Grandfather.

You see, the two men were great friends and were drinking together after a long absence between meetings. The beautiful young woman was along for the ride. After a long night of laughter and conversation, they argued about the woman. And instead of deciding on who gets her, and possibly ending their friendship, they shot her. The old woman said they thought more of their friendship than the love of a beautiful woman. The old woman found her in the corner with a hole in her forehead.

The old woman told this story to the constable when he arrived a few days later. There was only one officer of the law in a very large area and nothing was done about the incident. The young woman was buried close by and the two men were never named by the old woman. She was in fear of her life if she had told the officer.

Now that elder I told you about, the woman that told me this story, was one of the very young girls in the tent terrified throughout the whole incident. When she told me the story she still shivered when it came to the names of the men. By the writing of this book, that woman has passed on and the name of the other man will remain a secret.

Ken Marchand in front of petrified tree C & E

This picture was taken by a company called Cates & Erb, Inc. of Omak. They were logging near Inchelium and had some trouble with cutting a logging road into the hill side.

After some work was done they noticed the rock formation was not "bad rock" but a petrified tree. A substantial piece was broken off already and they began to watch for such problems and to avoid damaging more of these giant petrified trees.

Bob Erb said there were others in the area that you could see.   It is something that is rare in our area and we have not shown people where it is, the Tribe should make such decisions. I just thought it was an interesting piece of information you might like to know.

As you move north toward Riverside you should look off to the East from #97 and see a residential area and a saw mill. That is where our real village or town was located. There are ancient burial grounds there and it was told that the grass grew to the belly of a horse.

The next place to visit is Riverside, an interesting place and famous for the being the docking of the paddle wheel on the Okanogan River. It was a boom town and has settled into a very comfortable place to live. When you get to Riverside you can look north and see McLaughlin Canyon a few miles up the river. Between you and the canyon is a small falls in the river, today called Buttercup Falls.

This is Riverside and for a small community it was considered the hub of commerce for the north and south County. Riverside marked the head of navigation for stern-wheelers coming up the Okanogan River during spring runoff. You can still see the ring that the paddle wheel used to tie up at the bank to load and unload cargo.

The opening of the South half of the Colville Indian Reservation-to mineral entry in 1896 and to settlement in 1901-had made the place even more centrally located in terms of serving the central and northern parts of the county. Several earlier developments contributed to the establishment of Riverside.

One occurred in January, 1895, when a 635 acre allotment assigned to an Indian named John Salla Salla was terminated. This happened when the Columbia (Moses) reservation went out of existence. This made available for non-Indian to use more than a mile of land extending south from Johnson Creek along the west shore of the Okanogan River.

By 1897, promoters were designing an "Okanogan City" at the mouth of Johnson Creek. This venture failed. But, stern-wheelers continued to unload cargo at the site. A steamboat man, E.L. Hollenbeck reported there were "acres of freight" jamming a warehouse and tents, accumulating faster that teamsters could haul it away.

The place was then referred to as "Republic Landing" in thinly disguised effort to convince shippers that merchandise consigned to the booming mining camp of Republic could be economically dispatched to Johnson Creek. It was said the steamboat company promoting this scheme had alone amassed 35 tons of merchandise at the landing.

James E. Forde of the well known firm of Ellis and Forde at Loomis platted the Town of Riverside in 1902.　Lots were being sold and built on for three years before Forde's plat was filed with the county auditor in 1905.

A young attorney, William Compton Brown, who traveled by horseback from Republic across Pine creek to Conconully and attend a session of the superior court, returned by way of "Republic Landing" in May of 1899. These were his words:

"I rode from Conconully to the mouth of Johnson Creek over the established county road that is still there.　There was nothing where the town of Riverside afterwards developed.　But about a quarter or half a mile above where the bridge is today I came to the steamboat landing.　There was a sizable storehouse and wharf boat.　Instead of building wharves it was common in those days to make use of wharf boats moored to the river bank. There were also many indications about the place to show there must have been much activity when the boats were operating."

John Kendall (an early homesteader) was operating the ferry.　He told me that the steamboat would be coming in about ten days.　That spring was late and the river was too low for navigation. He explained to me that a new road was under construction and while it was still unfit for wagons I could make it by horseback. The new road went up and the east side of the river to where Keystone orchard is now. Then it took off into the hills and met the state road on Bonaparte Creek about seven miles east of present day Tonasket."

Riverside area looking east   ATM

After you leave Riverside a few miles you can look off to the East onto the mountains on the other side of the valley and see an undistinguishable draw with a road going half way up the draw.

That is the way to get to the place called Horse Slaughter Canyon. It was there that some farmers who were in a range fight with the ranchers chased a herd of horses off a cliff. You can see the bleached white bones from the air quite well, but you can get a better look if you go up the draw and look over the cliff yourself. The road is gated and permission is needed to get there, but it is possible to go and see for yourself.

You are about ten miles from Tonasket now and going through a place called Crumbacher Estates, a small development before you see the Janis Bridge. There was a story I heard a long time ago from a lady that worked for the Colville Tribes History Department. This is: "**The Way I Heard It**":

Along through this place there was a battle that lasted three days. The Chiefs had negotiators that could speak and translate what the Chiefs said and try to come to some conclusion and maybe a peaceful solution to the matter.

The Chiefs could not agree and the negotiators could not come to any agreements, and so the war was to begin. The Chiefs met on either side of a swale and set up camp. The battle was to begin in the morning.

As the sun rose in the sky, what looked like an equal number of warriors attacked each other in the swale. The battle lasted all day and as night fell the dead were removed and the death songs rang out into the night. The next two days were the same and war is not a pretty thing to watch.

The negotiators were working feverishly to end the war.

Then from out of the blue came a solution. One Chief who was very angry at the beginning of the war, decided to see if this solution could work. The other Chief that seemed to have acted in defense of his people was willing to listen.

"The solution was that one Chief agrees that he did not make a mistake in accusing the other Chief of wrong doing. The other Chief agree that he was right" and the war was over.

They both left the battle field and were looked upon with honor by their people.

To every story like this there is always a reason and a lesson to learn. Take your time and think, trying to hurt someone isn't the answer, if you take your time the answer will come.

As you go north a few miles you will be coming down the hill toward the Janis Bridge. Look off to your right, to the East, and you can almost see the battle field of McLaughlin Canyon. The dirt road going up the hill is the road to the battle site and the historical sign overlooking the battle field.

McLaughlin Canyon is a site of one of the famous battles between the trappers and traders and the Okanogan Indians. This is one version of that battle as told in 1891 by Mr. James McLaughlin the leader of the group caught at the canyon.

"It came near being a massacre. We started from the Wallula the latter part of June, 1858, with a pack train and one hundred and forty nine men for the Fraser River country.

The outfit comprised a representation from nearly all the states, and quite a number of half breeds. We got along peaceably with an occasional quarrel among the different sets of our men (which, of course, didn't count), until we arrived at Moses Canyon, where we were attacked by Red Jacket, a chief of the Palouse Indians.

In the fight we lost one man killed (Evans, of Portland), and several wounded, besides some of our pack animals. The reason we got off so lightly was that the Indians were anxious to stampede the stock, especially the pack animals, instead of hunting scalps.

We knew to a certainty that we were in for it for the rest of the journey and kept a bright lookout, and we were not disappointed. We had reached a point four miles above the mouth of the Okanogan, where we found the Indians reinforced by the Columbia's, or Rock Island Tribe, under Chief Moses, who took command of the combined Indian forces and tried to prevent our crossing.

Old French Way, as he was called, allowed us to take his canoes, and I crossed in the evening with twenty-one men to watch the movements of the Indians. I tell you there was no talking or sleeping that night. The next day we crossed the entire outfit and although we could see hundreds of painted devils, we were not attacked, and we camped that night at the mouth of Chiliwist Creek.

The next day Wilson of Portland, took command of the advance guard and we started along the east bank of the Okanogan River, keeping a bright lookout for ambushes, for the very quietness of the savages looked more dangerous to me than if they had been whooping and shouting at us. That night we were not molested and only one attempt was made to stampede the stock; but the next morning after we had climbed the first hill, before entering a canyon, not seeing any signs of the Indians.

I became suspicious and called a halt, while I rode forward with one man. I had not proceeded two hundred yards when I noticed bushes piled against rocks, and my eyes being pretty sharp, I noticed that the leaves were wilted. Telling my companion to stop where he was I started to investigate the suspicious circumstance, and had got within thirty yards when I noticed a painted buck behind a little stone fort, or breastwork and before I could investigate any further or bring my gun to my shoulder, he fired, the ball taking effect in the neck of my horse, killing him instantly.

The fight immediately became general, and lasted from 10 am until 5 pm, when we retreated to the river under a steady fire from the Indians.

We remained awake that night expecting an attack every moment. Several attempts were made during the night to stampede the stock, but as each attempt cost the reds some of their best braves, they desisted toward morning. We lost in the fight four killed and twenty wounded. The killed were McGrew, and Wright, of Cass Valley, California; one Irishman and one Englishman, whose names I have forgotten, also twenty five pack animals. Remember these events happened thirty-three years ago.

The next morning we built a raft of driftwood and crossed to the west side of the river. That is what they call the "Massacre of McLaughlin's Canyon" and it was hot for awhile. We were followed by the Indians all the way to Rock Creek, occasionally getting a crack at some thoughtless straggler."

Pictographs along the Okanogan HP

Look off to your left or northwest and you will see the white cliffs off in the distance. The hills around Tonasket have caves and some Indian writing and pictographs.

They tell of a cave that the Okanogan's used to escape the Blackfoot Indian raiders in the valley. The Blackfoot have the Okanagan in their traditional history, because we raided them and in return they are our traditional enemy.

When we heard of their coming, often the men were off on either a fishing or hunting trip, and in the summer the women were gone gathering roots and berries. The village was full of elders and children only. They had no defense and could only run and hide.

One cave near here could only be reached from the top of the hill. You had to crawl over the edge and down to the opening of the cave. The entrance could not be seen from the valley floor. As you entered the cave you went down a path along the wall of the cave. The cave could hold about 40 teepees and there were pictographs and signs along the cave walls describing the use of the cave for some time into the past. Fires could be lit and the cave was a constant comfortable temperature. An entire village could stay hidden there for many days with no discomfort. The raiders soon passed and the lookouts could see far up and down the valley, it was safe again.

The cave was sealed up and no sign was left to show an entrance. We are certain that vandalism would occur if it were left open to the public.

Chief Tonasket OBHS

Before you get to Tonasket the highway goes right through the place where the original village was, the town of Tonasket was a mile or two away. The town of Tonasket was named after a "chief" named Tonasket. He was not a hereditary chief as all of the Okanogan Chiefs were, but more of a self made chief. This is one of the stories about Chief Tonasket: **"The Way I Heard It":**

Tonasket became prominent in the following manner. In 1858 some of the Okanogans were fighting the whites who came overland with pack trains and horses via the Okanogan route to the newly discovered gold diggings in British Columbia. Many of the white parties were killed. Horses were also stampeded and stolen from them. Most of the fighting took place near the British Columbia line. In all there was never more that 70 or 80 Okanogan fighting and most of them had no guns. Tonasket was one their number.

Once they fought a large party of whites and stopped them from passing through. They had to retreat and change their direction. Then a still larger party of whites came on the scene.

The Indians set fires in the grass, one on the flanks of the party and another large fire ahead of them which spread into the trees. They separated and fired shots from behind the fires. The white party came to a halt and made ready for an attack. There were probably less than 20 Indians at this time while the whites must have numbered about 150.

Tonasket made himself leader of the Indians. He left half of his men here and there at the sides and front to shoot off their guns while he with the other rode down on the camp of the whites. The latter thought the Indians were going to attack them and prepared to shoot. Tonasket who was ahead held his gun above his head and called out "Don't Shoot, we are friends." He said to the whites, "I have great numbers of my warriors all around, to the sides and in front and behind you. They are waiting behind these fires. At my call they will come out and overwhelm you, but I do not want to do this. I want to be be your friend and treat you well, but I am chief of all this country and I want you to recognize me by paying some tribute for using and passing through my country."

The whites believed him; they wrote down his name and gave him many presents. He and his followers, then allowed them to pass on, gave them directions, and did not molest them any further. After this, other white parties recognized him as chief, not knowing any better, and always gave him presents. In this way Tonasket gained considerable influence and came to be called chief, although later the American Okanogan recognized him as such. Tonasket himself claimed to be head chief of the Okanogans who lived on the American side of the line, after the death of Chief Nicola, the Hereditary Chief of all the Okanogan People.

Tonasket can be credited with the fact that the town of Tonasket has a hospital and a school. When the agreement was being made for the Moses Reservation, from Wenatchee north along the Columbia River, the Okanogan River to the Canadian border on the East and Cascade Mountains to the West, present were Chief Sarsarpkin, Chief Tonasket, and Chief Moses, Tonasket was the one that demanded these things be included in the agreement.

Tonasket was a rancher and during the deadly cow killing winter of 1889-1890 he was one of the few that had hay put up prior to the winter to help feed his herd.

Early Cabin in Chewiliken Valley ANM

The next story has to do with the Chewiliken Valley to the east of where you are now. It was written in the Wenatchee World newspaper:

His name was Johnny Telkiah. He was a medicine man and Indians from the Colville Reservation and British Columbia reserves would attend ceremonies at his ranch in the Chewiliken Valley. During the long and cold winter months, "Chinook" dances were held there. These ceremonies, which sometimes lasted as long as eight days involved praying for good weather. Telkiah sang traditional songs during these events. Prior to each ceremony, he would fast and cleanse his body in the creek near his house after he had endured the hot vapors of his sweat lodge.

Telkiah was a man who could live in both worlds, Indian and white. He was also a successful rancher whose generosity towards those less fortunate than himself was well known. His sudden death on the advent of 1918 is unsolved and could have been due to foul play.

This story was told by Sarah Bone McCraigie, 82, born in 1904, and told by her son Jerry Eaneas, in the Okanogan Language, translated to English. She tells the story of the four years she spent with her uncle Johnny Telkiah.

Sarah begins: "During the early 1900s, most Indians spoke only their own tribe's language. There were not too many Indians who could speak and understand English.

Indian People taught their children how to work and perform indoor and outdoor chores. Children were taught how to work on the farm land, how to hunt wild game and catch fish. They never had a lot of time to play.

Parents taught their children how to pray to the Great Spirit and live like Indian Christians. The children also learned to honor, respect, and obey their elders. The ways and means of transportation during the early 1900s were, of course, by saddle horses and wagons pulled by the horse teams. There were some motor cars, but not many.

The father of Johnny Telkiah was Shwupkin. The father of Narcisse Bone Jim was Shweeyautkin. Shwupkin and Shweeyautkin were brothers by blood. And for this reason Johnny Telkiah and Narcisse Bone Jim were first cousins. Narcisse Bone Jim was my father, Johnny Telkiah was my uncle.

Johnny was born about the year 1862 and died January 1, 1918. Mary Magdalene Telkiah was Johnny's first wife. She was born about the year 1850 and she died about the year 1899 at 50 years of age.

Mary John was Johnny's half sister. She and Johnny had the same mother, Julia. Mary John was also half sister to Matilda Robinson and Pierre John. These had the same father. Matilda Robinson and her *brother, Pierre John, had land in the Similkameen Valley of the Southern British Columbia.*

Johnny Telkiah owned a house and a cattle ranch in the Chewiliken Valley. There he had his own cattle, work horses and race horses. The house is still standing today. It is located about 15 miles north of Riverside.

There is a small lake called Telkiah on what was once the northern end of Johnny's land. Johnny Telkiah also owned some farm land about seven miles north of Riverside on the west side of the Okanogan River, across from where the Keystone Orchard is today. Johnny would grow corn, potatoes, green beans, tomatoes and other crops.

She said, "I stayed and lived with my uncle Johnny Telkiah and my aunt Mary John on the cattle ranch in Chewiliken Valley and on the farm land west of the Okanogan River for about four years starting when I was a child of 10 years until I was 14. I could not speak and understand any English then.

At the Chewiliken Valley Cattle ranch my aunt Mary John taught me how to work and perform indoor and outdoor chores. I had to carry firewood into the house and build a fire in the kitchen stove so that Mary could cook. I also had to build a fire in the heating stove when the weather was cold. When we needed water, I carried in pails or buckets of it from the well.

On occasion, I would go with my uncle Johnny into the hills or mountains. We'd both ride saddle horses during these trips and he'd shoot and kill grouse. I'd place the birds in potato sacks and we'd pack them home to Mary who would prepare them for our meals.

There was a store or trading post in Riverside which carried food and clothing. At the store was a barn or stable for saddle or work horses and a parking area for wagons. Uncle Johnny used to go to the store for food and clothing. "I think Uncle Johnny had a lot of money which was kept safe in that trading post.

It was the last day of December 1917, and there was snow on the ground and the weather was cold. That morning Uncle Johnny mounted his saddle horse and left the Chewiliken Valley for that trading post in Riverside. There he withdrew a large sum of money and put it in a purse. He then rode home to the Chewiliken Valley.

After Johnny got home he said to Mary: "I have to make a journey to Republic. You'll have to get up early tomorrow morning to cook and prepare breakfast. And you'll have to feed the saddle horse some hay and grain." Early in the morning on January 1, 1918, my aunt Mary woke me up. She told me to go to the kitchen stove, build a fire, light the kerosene lantern and go to the barn and bring some hay and grain to the horses. I then put on my shoes and did these chores to prepare for Uncle Johnny's ride to Republic.

When I was done, I went back in the house where Mary was by now cooking breakfast. She looked at me and said, "Go to your Uncle Johnny's bedroom and wake him up. Breakfast is almost ready." I opened my Uncle Johnny's bedroom door and walked in. I saw my uncle Johnny lying on the bed. There was blood on his face. My uncle is having a nose bleed, I thought to myself. In a loud voice I said, "The breakfast is almost ready to eat." Then I walked back into the kitchen.

I think my aunt Mary told me about three times to wake Uncle Johnny up. Each time I went to his bedroom and noticed that he didn't move. Finally my aunt Mary told me to set the table which I did, and she walked into Johnny's room. I think she was there about two minutes or so. Aunt Mary then came out of the bedroom and I think she was crying.

She told me to sit down then she tied some potato sacks around my feet to keep them warm and told me to go to this white man's house to get help. Some of the current residents of the Chewiliken Valley say this white man may have been Louis Stafferson.

I began through the snow to this white man's house about a mile away. The white man was working by his barn. He tried to talk to me in English, but I couldn't understand. All I could say was Johnny! Come! Johnny! Come! We rode on his horse drawn sleigh to my Uncle Johnny's house. The White man and I walked in the door and saw my aunt Mary sitting by her bed on the floor, weeping. The white man tried to ask my aunt Mary questions, but she only knows a few words in English. She didn't say anything. She only pointed toward Johnny Telkiah's bedroom. When the white man went in the room and saw Johnny, he knew in a moment he was dead and got on the phone to the Indian Agent in Omak.

The Indian Agent spread the news of Johnny Telkiah's death among the Indians of the Colville Reservation. My Uncle David Isaac and another Indian named Pierre came to Johnny's house and prepared his body for the funeral and burial services. It was during the cleaning and preparation of his body that they discovered that his neck had been broken. Indian people who came to Johnny's house after he died searched for evidence. They found a set of cowboy boot prints on the ground next to Johnny's bedroom window. Some of the Indian people suspected that someone had been watching Johnny Telkiah when he left the Riverside trading post with a lot of money. If someone did, they may have followed him home.

Johnny Telkiah was buried at St. Mary's Mission. He had a son, Mike, who died in 1921 at age 29. Uncle Johnny Telkiah was a good man who helped everybody. I can't understand why the good men die and bad *ones live. Johnny Telkiah has been gone for over 68 years. His house he once lived in is uninhabited, boarded up and surrounded by weeds, a silent witness to his untimely death.*

When you get past Tonasket about five miles, you will notice a valley off to your left, to the west. Up that valley are Loomis, Nighthawk and Chopaka, along with Whitestone Lake, Spectacle Lake, Wannacut Lake, and Palmer Lakes (good fishing).

The next place you will see is Ellisforde, named after two Wenatchee business men Mr. Ellis and Mr. Forde, who opened a business there and the name stayed, they didn't. It was actually a permanent Okanogan Indian village (town). There is an Indian graveyard at the bottom of the hill behind the church. You will notice a kiosk, it has a very interesting history of the area and you should stop and read it.

Bell from the 1st Catholic Church   ANM

It was built by volunteers from the Oroville Catholic Church, and my father was one of those volunteers. There are many indicators of ancient life near here, for example, just over the hill to the east is an ancient pit house site and the people that own the land will not allow visitors to the site, even if you could find it. It is actually only visible from the air and only during certain times of the year.

Not far from here some ancient remains were found and reburied at the cemetery. One was from the 5th century and the other from the 13th century. There was a set of remains that was found and identified as the result of a raiding party. The injury to the back of the man was a very large hole, the woman had a similar wound and the child had head trauma. It is believed that the deaths were the result of a raid by one of our traditional enemies and this family was in the way.

You must remember that in ancient times the spear was a close combat weapon and was not a long throwing instrument. It had a large handle not longer than 5 feet or so and strong enough to hold the weight of a body off the ground. The trauma to the three Indians was quick and probably silent. During many excavations in the area fire pits, grave sites, and food caches have been found.

The area called Ellisforde area had permanent residents of more than 100 Okanogan Indians prior to 1800 and was a peaceful and restful place to stop visit relax and get something to eat during their travels up and down the valley. If you haven't noticed by now, most of our permanent encampments were less than days walking distance from each other and always on the East side of the river.

Loomis pre -1916   H. Gregg Photo-OBHS

If you traveled west up the small valley from Ellisforde you will come to a town called Loomis. It was a boom town during the mining hey days and there were cattle and cowboys.

There is a story of a real "cowboy" that lived up there in Loomis. Not many people remember him, but those that knew him do remember him. He was a true cowboy in every sense of the word. His life should have been a movie. This came out September 24, 1973, in the Wenatchee Daily World:

Loomis-Charlie Thorpe, 95 years old, son of Alvin Thorpe who came to the area before there was a town of Loomis, was buried at his birthplace recently.

Known at the closure of his life for "always a cowboy," there were periods where he was many

Charlie Thorp OBHS

other things, including being a section hand, a foot racer, homesteader, owner of a grey mare which was never outrun by any except

Hans Richter's Don Pedro, who, everyone knew, was once world champion quarter-mile horse.

He prospected with Tom Bean, hunted bighorn sheep as a boy in the Chopaka Valley, and at several times in his life was simply a man of leisure.

He also was noted for his keen eyesight.

Many are the tales of Charlie spotting the perfect camouflaged coyote and the elusive cougar. One time, while working for Claude Cutche, he called Mrs. Cutche out to the yard, and pointed miles away to the rim of Palmer Mountain. There, with the moon just rising behind him, was a buck deer standing in silhouette. On the day of the large funeral the question arose, and arguments ensued about precisely where Charlie was born, at Oroville, at Smith Point? Finally, there came shyly forward, Suzie, granddaughter of Indian Edwards. Said she: "His mother and Al were cutting wood up Sinlahekin Creek when Julia got sick and went home and had the baby." Julia and my grandmother were related. That seemed authentic enough to everybody.

So, on January 6, 1879, Charlie was born of Alvin Thorpe and his pureblood Indian wife, Julia, of Chief Sarsarpkin's Band. The log cabin still stands at the mouth of Toats Coulee Creek on land owned by John Woodard. There was one other child, Cecile, for whom the local creek is named, who died of pneumonia early in life. The Thorpe's were Virginians, frontiersmen all, and Alvin Thorpe stands out in Okanogan history for the antiquity of arrival. He went through the Caribou gold rush of 1859, ran a string of pack horses for Okanogan Smith, then settled in the Sinlahekin Valley long before a town grew there. He and three or four other white men lived with their Indian women in the valley, which teemed with wild life. Years later the mining era dawned.

Julius Loomis came from Massachusetts to give his name to a trading post around which a lively town grew after the discovery of gold in the hills. Al Thorpe was a familiar sight in the down town Loomis, selling his wagonloads of fresh farm produce.

He left the young half breed lad well fixed and it has been said that Charlie "went through" or "drank up" several good ranches. His early days were spent in Loomis and Palmer Mountain, at which time he was married to Nellie, a beautiful daughter of "Tenus" George Runnels. They had one child, Frances, a startlingly handsome girl, educated and launched socially in California by Charlie, but who came home finally to Oroville to die of the dreaded Consumption. It was as if he had several lives telescoped together. Around the age of 50 he married a young Chopaka woman, Edith Parker, and three children were born, resulting in another outstanding daughter of a different sort. This was Audrey, famous as a rodeo trick rider and professional jockey for seven years in the states and British Columbia. She adored her aged father and remained with him when the family was torn asunder and the two small brothers were adopted into other homes.

However, of all roles attached to Charlie in his many sectioned life, there is one which is the most universal and enduring; he was an old time fiddler. He fiddled for 50 years and more, loaded his violin case into a *buckboard or strapping it behind his saddle and riding to dances as far away as Colville and Brewster. No dance was complete without Nellie and Charlie being in attendance. And this was the heyday of the two young handsome, dark people.*

It began one winter when a young fellow Charlie's age spent the winter with Al Thorpe in Loomis, giving Charlie a few pointers on the violin. The boy was Phil Baker, father of the Phil Baker of early radio fame, whose whole family performed musically as a group. Charlie always played a number sort of classical "Waves of the Danube" by one J. Ivanovici, requiring some fancy bowing. It always stood out as a sort of hybrid among the regular, more virile repertoire such as "Chilliwack Slicker", "Alexander The One Man Band: or "Cheyenne."

He was genuine. The fiddle pointed due south and as he picked up the bow and bent forward, his high heeled boots began clumping out the rhythm and his music was as gay as birds cavorting in the sky on a windy summer night after several trips outside for purposes of limbering his playing, became slurred. The dance was ended when he began the tune "Me and the Fiddler's Doggone Tired"... Although in the thirties when a snappy number became popular, "Show Me the Way to Go Home" he switched to that. The latter was in the Chopaka days of the thirties when dances were staged at the schoolhouse, the abandoned Great Northern depot. The dust arose from the rough floor to which soft soap had been shaved earlier in the evening for slipperiness.

During these years when he lived at Chopaka, we all remembered a little nondescript buckskin horse which roamed the valley and could be caught up and ridden bareback a few miles by school children passing by. This was the horse, "Nespelem and Back" and it was a fact that Charlie had ridden him to Nespelem and back in a slow trot with scarcely a pause before the return trip was made. This was roughly around 200 miles.

Another story of Charlie was of the day when he was returning to Palmer Mountain after visiting the saloons of Loomis, and he teetered too far out of the saddle, so that the little sorrel mare he was breaking, threw him off. His foot caught in the stirrup and she tore up through the canyon. "As luck would have it," Charlie always related, "on that day Claude House had strung a new barbed wire fence. She hit this with such force it threw her back and my foot came loose. So I just sat me down on a rock there and thought, "A man doesn't die till his time comes."

He also told of riding through McLaughlin Canyon with his father and old Chief Sarsarpkin when a boy of ten and having the chief take them over the battleground and point out the rock embattlements, the strategic points of the famous massacre where he had fought. It was at the autumn of his life, when he was in his seventies and eighties, that he became a cowboy for the Robert Fancher. He knows cows.

He could seemingly place himself in their position and know what they were going to do.

Like the day he nonchalantly came driving into the camp a steer used in the spring as roping practice that had grown leery of men and horses. He dropped the animal outside the gate went into his supper and it took six riders to corral the critter! "It was a pleasure to watch him work cattle," said Mrs. Fancher, and she would sit in the car and watch Charlie bringing in 300 head of cows with their calves down the steep Cecile Creek trail calmly working his cud of "snoose" behind his lower lip.

Cattle in Okanogan country ANM

The Okanogan is cattle country. This book would not be complete without something about the industry and how it started here. This story came from the Okanogan County Heritage, June 1963:

"One hundred years ago this past spring, a herd of cattle moved slowly up the West side of the Okanogan River. There were two hundred head of scrubby, long horned Spanish stock. The grass on the hill sides was lush and green. Still, a boiling contrail of dust marked the herd's advance.

Driven by lean, sun-blackened cowboys, the cattle had struggled across the Columbia River near present day Bridgeport. It took them 10 days to pass through Okanogan country. The herd forded the Okanogan River just south of its confluence with the Similkameen and was hurried past the swamps bordering Lake Osoyoos. Three years earlier, in 1860, Ben Snipes had lost 18 head in these swamps because of stampedes caused by unbearable swarms of mosquitoes. Now he was wiser.

In British Columbia his herd followed the Okanogan lakes picked up the Thompson River, and swung northward towards Barkerville in the Caribou gold fields. There, winter weary miners paid an average of $100 a head for cattle which had cost Snipes $6 to $16 in Oregon's Willamette Valley. With nearly $100,000 in gold dust, the young cattleman's return trip to the Dalles was nearly as nerve racking as the northward drive had been. Every cluster of brush might signal an ambush in this wild and lawless country. But Snipes reached home safely with the capital he needed to *expand. Within a few years, people called him the Cattle King of the Northwest.*

These great cattle drives up the Caribou Trail by Snipes and others marked the beginning of the history of the livestock industry in Okanogan County. Herds had grazed here earlier, but they belonged to settlers in the Canadian Okanagan, at the time when the first settler in the Similkameen Valley, and Judge John C Haines, later customs officer at Osoyoos, probably grazed as far south as the Columbia.

In the mid-1850's came the electrifying gold strikes along the Fraser River and farther north in the Caribou. Prospectors arrived by the boatload at Victoria. Others hurried up the Okanogan valley. The demand for beef in the far-flung mining camps swiftly outran the local supply. So each spring, for about 10 years, herds trailed north from The Dalles, the Yakima country and Walla Walla. Everyone who watches television has heard of the Chisolm Trail. Yet the Caribou Trail, 600 miles from the Dalles to the northern gold camps, was twice as long as the Chisolm and of greater concern to the cowboys; where the Chisolm led from the plains of Texas to "civilization" at the Kansas railheads, the Caribou twisted into an unknown and hostile wilderness.

Snipes made his first drive as a lad of 20 in 1856. One year he wintered 500 head near Lake Osoyoos. That spring he brought the first beef into Williams Lake and pocketed premium prices of $150 a head. Expenses were light. White cowboys cost a dollar a day, Indian riders came for almost nothing. The duty into Canada, once customs was established, amounted to two dollars a head. Dan Drumheller drove cattle up the Caribou Trail from Walla Walla. One of his herds was stampeded by camels experimentally used by Canadian officials to pack supplies up the Fraser River.

A.J. (Jack) Spawn, 16 years old, came trailing up the Caribou in 1861 with a herd owned by Major John Thorpe of Yakima. One evening near Loup Loup Creek, Spawn crouched behind bushes to watch Indian toss a white scalp about as they danced.

Small bands of natives tried repeatedly to drive off part of Thorpe's herd. At the mouth of Johnson Creek Spawn shot one of the marauders. The situation got sticky, but friendly Chief Tonasket escorted the party to Lake Osoyoos. Spawn, later to become a well known cattle buyer in Okanogan County, took part in several other drives, usually as a supervisor rather than owner. In 1868, the year of the last drive to the Caribou, Spawn fled from "suspicious characters" in a mining camp and with his saddle bags filled with gold dust rode without food and virtually without sleep from British Columbia to The Dalles before finding help.

Of all the prospectors drifting north through the Okanogan only one had settled here. He was Hiram J. (Okanogan) Smith, who established a trading post at Lake Osoyoos in 1858. (His Grandson, Bob Irwin, still lives in Oroville and is a very interesting person to know.) Smith prospected, planted the first apple orchard in what later became Washington territory, provided a haven for travelers, and ran horses and about a hundred beef cattle (mainly for his own supply) to qualify as Okanogan County's first cattleman. His brand was a numeral 3. This represented a backwards "E" taken from the last name of Smith's son-in-law, Jack Evans.

There are many more people that made up the cattle industry in Okanogan County and they can be investigated at the Okanogan County Museum at Okanogan. They are a fine group of people that are always willing to help.

Oroville 1920's   H. Gregg Photo - OBHS

Oroville is the last stop on our journey through the USA and Indian Country.

I have found that from here to Enderby is a long historically diverse way to go. I will have to find the time to continue the rest of this journey later, in another like kind of book. I will give you a glimpse into the Okanagan north through the Similkameen-Okanagan Region, the Central and North Okanagan. I will start with Oroville because it is a place that seemed to be the cross roads of People traveling north, south, east or west, you had to go through Oroville and Lake Osoyoos.

The Okanogan People that lived here were to the east of Osoyoos Lake between two streams below what is now the airport. Another group lived a distance from them a few miles South. Before the coming of the white man there were as many as 400 that lived in the area and an equal amount above the head of Lake Osoyoos, they were called the NKMIP, "the People from the bottom of the lake," (a term translated to mean they lived at the last lake in the valley). Osoyoos has a meaning like, "Narrowing of the waters". There was a time in the 1800's when the lake was so low that you could literally cross it without getting your knees wet.

Oroville's first white man in the current city limits was Alex McCaulley in about 1873 and he lived at the south end of Oroville in "Rag town", or tent city. It was a gold rush town that had more saloons than homes and an interesting early life.

"Rag Town"   OBHS

Oroville, a town whose Okanogan name is Salti'lxu' (heaping stone house). This is the story behind the name.

There was a well-known Chief Pelkamu'lox, he was born about 1705 or 1710, and we are not sure but pretty close to that time. He became a noted Chief and was known for many, many of his daring deeds and his political prowess. He was known far and wide throughout the country, and I don't use the country as BC or Washington, I mean "Indian Country."

During the early part of his life, there was a lot of war. We think that these wars commenced in his father's time or before, probably it continued for many years before he became Chief. Many Okanagan's as well people from other tribes have been killed.

Salti'lxu', (Oroville) which is the place of his headquarters. It was the Chief's seat of government for the Okanagan Tribes. The old name of the place was Okana'quen; Pelkamu'lox built for him a stone parapet and made it into a fort. The place became known as Salti'lxu', "Heaping Stone House".

It is said there was also a cave near there, the approach to which was defended with breastworks of stones. In case of necessity the people took refuge in it, and from there no party could approach, except under cover of night, without being observed. This place is said to have been impregnable and war parties of Thompson, Shu Shwap, Kutenai, and others assaulted it were easily beaten off.

Kwoli' la, the Kamloops chief, had heard of the many attacks by enemy war parties on Pelkamu'lox and determined to go and see him. His people tried to dissuade him, telling him it was very dangerous for anyone to visit him, for his people had been attacked so often that they trusted no one and attacked all strangers on sight who approached their place. Seeing that Kwoli' la was determined to go, the Shwap and the people of Nkama'peleks, who at that time were a mixture of Shu Shwap and Okanogan, offered to accompany him in an armed body, but he refused their offer, saying he would go alone.

As he was leaving, his people told him, "Pelkamu'lox, people will kill you before they know who you are, and even if they know, they may kill you". Kwoli' la answered, "I am Pelkamu'lox brother, and will go and see him alone."   Arriving on the open ground before Pelkamu'lox's house, the people ran out to meet him in battle array. Pelkamu'lox recognized him and was glad to see him.

He took him to his house and kept him as his guest for a long time. Kwoli' la advised Pelkamu'lox to forsake Sali' lxu' and go north with him. He told him, "Sali' lxu'" is a bad place to live in. You will always have trouble as long as you stay there." Pelkamu'lox was persuaded. It was early summer, and he and his people traveled north with Kwoli 'la to Komkena'tko, "headwaters", now called Fish Lake, in the Nicola Country.

This place was, at that time, in Shu Shwap territory, for the Shu Shwap claimed the country south of Kamloops around the head of Nicola River. Stump Lake, Douglas Lake, Fish Lake, and Chaperon Lake, were all in Shu Shwap country. This country, at that time, was full of elk and deer, and there were also many sheep, bear, and other game. Prairie chicken, grouse of all kinds, and water fowl were plentiful, and the lakes teemed with fish. Here at Fish Lake Kwoli 'la made a lasting agreement with Pelkamu'lox, giving him the perpetual use over all the Shu Shwap territory of the upper Nicola Valley, south east, and west of Chaperon Lake, comprising Douglas Lake and Fish Lake. The "Stuwi'xemux" and

Ntlakya'pamux held the country west and south around Nicola Lake and Minnie Lake to the Similkameen.

Kwoli 'la said, "You will have the country for yourself and your people as your own. I will live as your neighbor at Toxoxi'ten (Chaperon Lake) and will retain all the country from there north. You will make Fish Lake your headquarters in the summer and I will summer at Chaperon Lake so that we may be close neighbors part of each year. You will give me your daughter, Kokoimalks to be my foster child and she will always live with me, but your son you will keep with yourself." Pelkamu'lox had only two children at this time, both of them very young.

After this Pelkamu'lox and most of his people spent their summers in their new country with headquarters around Fish Lake and Douglas Lake, and in the wintertime lived at Nkama'peleks. Henceforth Salti'lxu was deserted of permanent inhabitants and was no longer the main village of the Okanagan. Those people who did not go with Pelkamu'lox moved north to different parts of the Okanagan Lake country and especially to the head of the lake around Nkama'peleks band, which were now much mixed with them, began to winter around Douglas Lake and Fish Lake, forming as it were a new band. However, even up to the present day they look upon themselves as merely an offshoot of the Nkama'peleks and Okanagan people and as really one with them.

Each year when Pelkamu'lox left for his winter quarters at Nkama'peleks, Kwoli 'la at the same time left to winter at Kamloops. Being head chief of the Okanagan, Pelkamu'lox often traveled to all the bands of the tribe, visiting first here and then there. He also traveled extensively among the neighboring tribes, visiting the Stew's, Upper Thompson, Shu Shwap of Kamloops, and it is said, the Wenatchee, Columbia, SanPoil, Spokane, and Kalispell. He went a number of times buffalo hunting to the plains, by way of the Flathead country, and was therefore well acquainted with chiefs and people of all the tribes to the south and east as far as the Coeur d'Alene, Nez Perce, Walla Walla, Yakama, Kutenai, Shoshoni and Blackfoot.

On his trip the party met near Helena, Montana, the first white men they had seen (Legace and MacDonald, explorers and trappers of the Northwest Co.). On the return trip these men accompanied the party as far west as the Columbia River, where they wintered with the Colville chief.

After Pelkamu'lox traveled around in his own country and within the borders of the neighboring tribes, telling of the wonderful men he had seen on his recent trip. Kwoli 'la invited him to Kamloops to tell of the event. He accompanied the Shu Shwap to their salmon fishing and trading rendezvous at Pavilion and Fountain, on Fraser River. Here he was mortally wounded by an arrow, in an altercation with a Lillooet chief. When dying he charged Kwoli'la with the guardianship of his son, Hwistesmexe'qen, and asked him to see that he avenged his death.

For full particulars of this part of the history of Pelkamu'lox, see Dawson, "The Shu Shwap People," pp. 26 27; and Wade, "The Thompson Country" pp. 13-15

HEE HEE Stone

The Molson Highway has a historical spot at the summit called the "Hee Hee Stone". It came from a story of our People long before contact. The Hee Hee Stone looked like a young Indian Girl facing west toward the Chopaka Mountains. It was a place where travelers would leave gifts and stop a moment to pray and give thanks before continuing their journey.

It is said that the statue "looking" rock formation was incredibly life like. Around the turn of the century a group of miners blew it up.

— Tuesday, Nov. 12, 1963   THE WENATCHEE DAILY WORLD

THE HEE-HEE STONE — A group of grizzled cowboys pose beside the famous landmark, after its dynamiting in 1905. Directly behind the stone (fourth person from left) sits "Tenas" George Runnels, notable miner, homesteader, squawman of the early days. This rare photo was loaned from the collection of the late Val Haynes of Osoyoos, B.C., who died last year at the age of 85.

Wenatchee Daily World, Tuesday, November 12, 1963.

"THE HEE-HEE STONE--A group of grizzled cowboys pose beside the famous landmark, after its dynamiting 1905. Directly behind the stone (fourth person from left) sits "Tenas" George Runnels, notable miner, homesteader, squawman (sic) of the early days. This rare photo was loaded from the collection of the late Val Haynes of Osoyoos, B.C., who died last year at the age of 85."

"The Hee Hee Stone"

Blue Flower was a beautiful maiden who lived in what is now Northeastern Washington. Her father was a chief of the Kalispell tribe.

One day, Blue Flower filled her basket with camas and started West, towards the Okanogan country. She knew that a handsome young warrior by the name of Scrakan lived in the Okanogan Country. He was the middle one of three brothers, all of whom were great warriors. The girl hoped that Scrakan would like her and that he would ask her to be his wife.

Blue Flower climbed the mountain range west of her country and saw the Okanogan country spread out before her. Wanting to look her best when she first appeared, she stopped to make herself beautiful. She took her shell comb from her basket, and combed her long hair so she would braid it more smoothly. She painted her face with paint made from red clay.

Soon, she saw the three brothers hurrying to meet her. In a dream they had learned of her coming, and at daybreak had started out to greet her. When they saw how beautiful she was, each of them asked her to be his wife. In their jealousy, the two younger brothers fought.

Coyote came along and saw them fighting and laughed. He thought it funny that two brothers should knock and kick each other because of a girl. His laughter annoyed Blue Flower, and she spoke sharply to him. Then Coyote became angry. "I'll get even with you," he said. "I permit no one to speak sharply to me."

Coyote made his powers and turned the lower part of the girl's body into stone. He made his powers again and moved the three brothers back to where they had been when they had their dream. Then he turned them into three mountains.

When he came back to Blue Flower, he found that she had thrown the basket of camas back into the land of the Kalispell.

She wanted no camas to grow in the land of the Okanogan People. Then she sang her power song and changed the rest of herself into stone.

Coyote turned to her and gave her special power, "You will help the people who are to come. You will be a wishing stone. People will bring you gifts, and you will make their wishes come true."

Then, he faced the three mountains west of him and made three laws. To the one in the middle he said, "You will remain a sharp-pointed peak without shoulders. The women will always like you, just as this Kalispell girl did. They will take pieces of your body, to make ornament s for their bodies. The new people who are to come will call the pieces copper."

To the oldest brother Coyote said, "Because you did not fight with the others you will always stand with your head and shoulders high and proud. You will always be known as Big Chopaka Mountain. People will be able to see you for a long distance."

To the youngest brother he said, "Because you were beaten and laid upon the ground in the fight, you will be a low mountain forever. You will never raise your head high again."

To this day the three mountains stand where Coyote transformed them.

Drawing by Arnie Marchand

For many generations the Kalispell plain were blue with camas in the spring, and when the camas was through blooming, Indians came from far and near to dig the camas bulb.

For many generations the maiden stood near the place where she stopped to paint her face and braid her hair. The Okanogan People called her "Enamtues", which means sitting on the summit.

Chesaw pre 1902

The town of Chesaw is near here having the distinction of being the only town in the state named after a Chinaman. On July 21, 1890, Father de Rouge recorded that he baptized Johnny Chinaman at the Kettle River. The sponsor was Chief Antoine. The real name of this Chinaman was Joseph Chee Saw.

Oroville has many interesting places to visit nearby. The Molson Museum, Chesaw, Havillah are all very nice drives.

The Ranald McDonald grave site and mural can be seen on the West Kettle River Road prior to the turn off to the Midway Bridge.

The mural was built by the Job Corp and text written by Mary Warring, and financed jointly by the Ferry County Historical Society and the Ferry County Commissioners. The mural is a community achievement.

The mural consists of three 8'x4' panels which depict the life Ranald McDonald who was the son of Archibald McDonald, chief factor of the Hudson Bay Company and Princess Raven, daughter of Chief Comcomly of the Chinook Tribe. Ranald, a 19th century adventurer, deliberately capsized a small boat in the waters off the coast of Northern Hokkaido during the Takagawa Shogunate in 1848. Taken prisoner on his arrival on Rishiri Island, he was transferred by junk to Nagasaki where he was tried for violating Japanese exclusionary edicts. Ranald was sentenced to imprisonment in a small living area but encouraged to teach English to a highly trained, select group of 14 Dutch speaking translators who were anxious to learn English. Respected by the Japanese as their first teacher English, his pupils played significant roles as translators during the visits of Commodore Perry, and the resulting trade negotiations between Japan and the United States.

Confined for nearly a year, the Japanese authorities released Ranald to Commander Glenn of the USS Preble in 1849. He was returned to Shanghai where he once more continued his wanderings as a sailor, later miner, and rancher. He was active in the gold fields of Australia, Vancouver Island, the Caribou and Horsefly Country.

Ranald retired at Hudson Bay's abandoned Fort Colville where along with his cousin Donald McDonald, they preempted claims on former Hudson Bay territory. While on a visit to his niece Jenny Nelson (later Lynch) near Toroda Creek on the Colville Reservation, his health deteriorated, and he died in her arms in 1894, Ronald's grave, now a State Historical Monument, is located in an Indian Cemetery on Customs Road, Curlew.

Medicine Lake near Oroville   ANM

This is a picture of a medicine lake just northwest of Oroville. The local historians say that a man named Ripley "discovered" the lake and found it to be of great help to people with arthritis, joint pain and such. **"The Way I Heard It":**

An old Indian man came riding into the camp near Oroville and could not get off his horse, and after a time was helped down. He was very old and could not move very well without help. He said he was going to the medicine lake on the hill and would be there for some time. After a short time they helped him back on his horse and he left. A few weeks later he came riding back into the camp, got off his horse without help and sat and talked for awhile. He said the lake had strong medicine and was very warm and you could bath in it for a long time, but be careful, if you sank too deep you would be burned.

He said he was traveling back to his home up north, rose, walked quickly to his horse and jumped up on the mount and rode off at a quick trot.

I do believe that Mr. Ripley did go up and see the small lake of medicine, but I wonder if he really "discovered" it.

General Sherman public domain

This next story came to me from a friend, Mr. Wilbur G. Hallauer of Oroville. My parents worked for him when I was a kid and they really respected him. I, too, have great respect for him, as I have come to know him. He was a State Senator, local business man, historian and entrepreneur, and author of "CHADS: From a Diverse Life" and "CHADS: From a Diverse Life II."

His life is the Okanogan and his books are at the Okanogan Borderland Historical Society's museum called "The Depot". It is Oroville's tourist information center and is housed in one of two of the last Great Northern Railroad depots of its style in the state of Washington.

The story is in the "Travel Accounts of General William T. Sherman to Spokane Falls, Washington Territory, in the Summers of 1877 and 1883" by William Tecumseh Sherman and Philip Henry Sheridan, published by Ye Galleon Press, Fairfield, Washington.

I want to begin on August 7th under "Reports of Inspection," made in the summer of 1883.

We pick up the journal coming from Kettle Falls across the mountains to Okanogan Country on their way to the Fraser River and Hope, B.C. I found it very interesting and I truly hope it is of some interest to you. The party has journeyed by train also and has on at least one occasion been in the presence of Chief Moses and Chief Tonasket before this part of their journey.

> *"Our party, as organized for the march to Fraser River, consisted of 81 persons, 66 horses, and 79 mules, General Sherman's mess consisted, as before, of himself, Justice Gray, Colonel Dodge, and myself, General Miles had with him Surgeon Moore, Lieutenant Mallery (his aide), and Mr.*

Saurin; Major Jackson, commanding the escort, Lieutenant Rowell, Backus, Abercrombie, and Goethals. Backus was in charge of the pack trail, and Goethals was the engineer officer and general guide; he, having been over the country before, had prepared a most accurate map and description of the route.

We were provided with tents, the poles of which had been cut and so jointed as to be readily carried on mules. The little personal baggage we had was prepared so as to be readily carried in the same way. Good strong horses had been selected for our riding purposes.

August 8- In the early morning we took an Indian trail leading up Kettle River, passing through heavy forest, over some rough spurs of hills, and across sandy, low ground; here and there were Indian cabins and small fields of cultivated land. In our march the General led off, except occasionally, when someone would go ahead as guide; then followed the rest of us in Indian file; after which came our cavalry escort, and finally our pack train; the latter under charge of skillful packers mounted on mules.

This country is infested with a small fly or gnat which is a torment to both man and brute. There is no escape from its pertinacity except by the most industrious application of a leafy bush, and as our party wound along, each one with a bush in hand, we resembled a church procession on Palm Sunday.

Following up Kettle River for about 7 miles we crossed over to the right bank, and leaving it, took a northwest direction over the rugged spur of a mountain to Deadman's Creek, which we followed up a mile or so and made camp on the best ground we could find in the mountain gorge through which the creek flows. Kettle River here makes a great bend, and sweeping around across the national boundary line.

A train follows around this bend, but as it crosses the river many times, is not passable except at low stages of water, when the river is fordable; otherwise it is said to be reasonably good trail, and was formerly considerably used by Hudson Bays Company people. The trail we were following cuts across the bend 30 miles, and is known as Little Mountain Trail.

Considerably south of this is another trail, known as the Old Hudson Bay Company Trail.

All of these trails have been but little used of late years, and have become greatly obstructed with fallen timber. A couple of companies of infantry from Coeur d'Alene had been out since about the middle of June re-opening the southernmost of them, but as this was not the one over which General Sherman wished to travel they were changed over to the Little Mountain Trail, but owing to want of time or energy on the part of the commanding officer they had done but little towards improving it.

In consequence of this Lieutenant Abercrombie, with a detachment of Jackson's cavalry, had been dispatched ahead of us to do what he could to open the route. He however could do little more than keep ahead of us. Caches of oats had been made along the trail at proper distances from camps; one of these was at the point on Deadman's Creek where we now encamped.

August 10 - This morning we continued on down the mountain over a comparatively good trail. Near the foot of the mountain we

152

again came to Kettle River, which we crossed at a good ford, and, continued up its valley for about 10 miles, crossed and recrossed it several times, the last crossing was near the mouth of Tenasket Creek. *(note: this creek is really on the east side of Osoyoos Lake)*

Along this part of the river the trail occasionally passes over sharp points of hills overlooking the stream, but generally the land is level and rolling. The river is lined with large cottonwood trees, rather a rare sight of late. The country is well covered with grass, and the scenery is fine. Near the mouth of the Tenasket are a couple of houses built by a white man known as Buckskin John, but now owned by Chief Tenasket, who lives at Osoyoos Lake, but uses these ranches for his cattle herds. There are also here several fields enclosed with good worn fences.

August 11 - As the trail today leads through a bad strip of fallen timber, we did not leave camp until 8 o'clock in the morning, thus giving time to Lieutenant Goethals with a pioneer party to cut it out. The trail leads up the narrow valley of the

Tenasket for 3 or 4 miles, passing through the before-mentioned strip of obstructed road; it then leads over the divide to Myers Creek, another tributary of the Kettle River. This divide is a mountain about 1500 feet above the creek.

The side upon which we ascended was very steep and in on long stretch. The descent was long and sloping, and covered with a fine forest of pines. Soon after reaching the foot of the mountain we came to Myers Creek, a good sized mill stream, edged with willows, cottonwood, and a great variety of berry bearing bushes.

Here we found a couple ambulances and wagons which had been sent from Lake Osoyoos to meet us. From Osoyoos here there is an old road or trail formerly used for reaching gold mines about 20 miles north of here on Kettle River. During this day we made 16 miles. The scenery was fine, but much obscured by smoke.

August 12 - The trail does not follow Myers' Creek, but, after crossing it passes directly over the divide to the watershed of the Okinakane. This divide, although containing many short steep pinches, is not difficult nor high. To Osoyoos Lake is 18 miles, most of the way without timber. The country is rolling and mostly covered with grass, large areas of which had been recently burnt. There was no water the entire distance except in two pools, on of which was too alkaline for use and the other somewhat difficult to reach by reason of swampy margin.

In approaching the Okinakane we passed some Indian ranches with small fields about them. Soon after midday we reached Osoyoos Lake, where is located a United States custom house, the principal business of which is to collect $1 per head on cattle imported across the boundary from British Columbia. The custom house is a log cabin shanty with dirt roof, and a small and similar attachment serving the purpose of kitchen. This squalid establishment stands unenclosed by fence in the midst of sand and dirt, on the edge of a ravine containing a fine spring of cool water, the only redeeming feature about the place.

In front of the house, upon a crooked stick, waved the stars and stripes, below which emblems of sovereignty was the revenue flag. The collector, Mr. C.B. Bash, living here alone was very courteous to us. The day was exceedingly hot and oppressive, and although so unattractive, his house furnished us cool shelter from the scorching sun. On the low ground next the lake is the ranch of Mr. Smith surrounded with patches of cultivation and fruit trees. From him we obtained melons and apples, the latter of a most excellent flavor. Smith keeps a sort of store, trading principally with Indians.

Osoyoos Lake is a strip of water resembling a good sized river; it is in fact only the widening out of the Okinakane, which leaving the lake at its southern extremity, flows sluggishly to find its way to the Columbia. The lake is surrounded at the distance of 2 or 3 miles by mountains and hills. The intervening space is a sloping plain of sand and sage brush. Around the edges of the lake are tule marshes. The water is clear and shores sandy. The region round about is quite destitute of timber and the whole aspect is one of barrenness. In 1860 or 1861 the hull a steamboat was built on this lake and floated down the Okinakane to ply upon the Columbia above The Dalles.

About the same time Mr. Gray and other Oregon pioneers, with the restlessness characteristic of that class, leaving the smiling lands of Oregon, penetrated with their families to this inhospitable region. After a short sojourn they returned wiser if not better people.

We pitched our camp on a high bluff overlooking the custom house or shanty and close by the camp of a company of the Twenty-first Infantry here on temporary duty from Vancouver barracks, taking care of a quantity of forage sent here for our use. During the afternoon the General was called upon by Tenasket and a large following of his people. He is a respectable looking oldish man, resembling in appearance a Louisiana Creole planter. He is said to be quite wealthy in cattle and farms. In the night a strong wind sprang up covering everything with dirt, sand and disgust.

August 13 - We were glad to leave this disagreeable place, and so too, evidently were the infantry soldiers who were early in the morning breaking camp preparing to their leaving for Vancouver. The company proposed to float down the Okinakane on rafts in preference to a hard march overland.

The pinkeye had made its appearance among the cavalry horses, and such of them as were affected were left behind with some of the men under Lieutenant Abercrombie to await the return of the troop after having made the trip to Frazer River.

We took the road leading up the lake through deep sand, sage-brush, and grease-weed. About 2 miles from the custom-house we crossed the northern boundary line of the United States and entered upon British territory. The boundary line is marked near the lake by a pyramid of stones.

Crossing this line recalls the controversy some forty years since had over the Oregon question, which controversy came nigh involving two great nations in war. At that time, the entire country from the northern boundary of California to the Russian possessions was called Oregon. The United States became owners of it in 1804 by purchase from the French Government. The latter had acquired it by treaty from Spain, which Government had established her claim to it by discovery and occupation.

The British claimed it from Spain in satisfaction for certain damages alleged to have been sustained by on Mears, a half-pay lieutenant of the British navy, who, in 1790, to evade certain maritime regulations of his own country, and also of Spain, sailed with fraudulent papers from a Portuguese port in the East Indies, bound on a trading expedition to Nootka Sound, an insignificant bay on the west coast of Vancouver Island. He was expelled from there by the Spanish authorities, and then land before his own government a bill for damages. The British Government, seeing in them an opportunity for seizing on a country, backed up his pretensions with gigantic preparations for was against Spain. The latter nation being entangled with complications growing out of Napoleon's schemes, was in no condition to resist, and granted to Great Britain certain trading privileges upon the Northwest coast of America.

This was the celebrated Nootka convention. These privileges were carefully nursed, and in time grew into the color of ownership to the whole country down to and including the Columbia River.

In 1843 people form the United States began to settle in Oregon and the great fertility of the country and salubrity of the climate becoming known attracted in a few years a large population. The Hudson Bay Company held sway over the country under British grants, and conflicting interests soon made it necessary to settle the question jurisdiction. The controversy between the British Government and that of the United States was long and spirited. The British threatened to maintain their claims by resort to war. During to political campaign which resulted in the election of Mr. Polk to the Presidency the question resistance to British assumptions entered largely into the spirit of the election contest, and "Fifty-Four Forty, or Fight", coupled with "Texas regardless of consequences," became the political slogan. The result was the annexation of Texas, but the fear of then ruling portion of the United States that by extending northward too much non-slavery holding States might spring up caused the claim to the parallel of 54'40' to be abandoned.

One of the first acts of the new President was to propose to the British Government to *compromise on the 49th parallel. This the British Government at first indignantly declined, but at length an agreement was effected, accepting the forty-ninth parallel as the dividing boundary, but giving to Great Britain the whole of the island Vancouver.*

About 2 miles beyond this noted line we came to the residence of Judge J.C. Hayne, the British collector of customs. Unlike the custom-house on the other side of the line, this is a neat, comfortable frame building, with brick chimneys and broad piazzas. It occupies a beautiful site on the shore of the lake, which is here a clean sandy beach. Judge Hayne received us most hospitably; his wife and family were absent at Westminster. At this point is a narrow place in the lake, making it, in fact, two lakes. Over this neck is a rude bridge reaching the British custom house we met a half dozen of Chinamen who being about to enter the territory of the United States contrary of the law excluding Chinese, were turned back by the United States collector to retrace the dreary road to the Frazier River.

Crossing the bridge just mentioned we continued up the shore of the lake for about 4 miles, and turning to the left, ascended the divide between the lake and the Similkameen River. This divide is not very high, but it is very steep and rough; the descent is gradual, following down a narrow valley or canyon for several miles. On either hand, are high mountains and several small lakes are passed on the way. These contain putrid water, smelling badly.

After the descent we came abruptly upon the Similkameen, a stream in size between a creek and river. We traveled up it for 7 or 8 miles and then went into camp on its steep and high bank. Just before reaching this point the river washes close under the point of a mountain; around this point the trail has been cut from the solid rock and is supported by a substantial wall. This was the work of British troops engaged on the boundary survey. Although the sun was hot we had a good breeze and did not suffer; nor were we tormented by gnats and mosquitoes.

The place where we encamped was a smooth plain, gently sloping from the foot of a bare mountain. This plain had no grass, but plenty of cactus in bunches. The atmosphere continues smoky, obscuring much fine scenery.

August 14 - Within about 2 miles after resuming our trail this morning we came to an extensive scope of meadow land, causing us to regret that we had not continued on and encamped at this place. A few miles further brought us to ranches with large fields of oats, wheat, and grass, with gardens of corn, potatoes, and other vegetables. The chief of these places was that of Mr. Richter, who was at this time putting up large ricks of hay; he had large quantities of it still on hand from last year.

The people who cultivate these farms appear to know but little of modern improvements in way farming implements. Their wagons are rough affairs with solid wooden wheels like Mexican carretas. Passing through this cultivated belt we came to Price Mill, the site of an old Hudson Bay trading post.

The valley is enclosed by high mountains, which, above the mill, gradually close together, often making narrow places between the mountains and river, which are exceedingly rough by reason of the rock and stones which have fallen from the mountain.

The mountains are exceeding precipitous, in fact, in places quite perpendicular. In many places occur stone slides which are very curious they look as though rocks had been poured out from above, and, like sand, had assumed a natural slope; the rocks are of every dimension from a paving stone up to a good sized building block; the large ones, sometimes the size a street car, falling with great power roll to a greater distance from the foot of the mountain. The formation is conglomerate and trap, alternating every now and then with granite. Clinging to the sides of the mountains is a sparse growth of pines, and along the river a thicket of cottonwood and willows.

August 15 - Our trail upon starting let close under the foot of the mountain, which, rising high above us to the east, kept the sun from us until late in the morning. The valley gradually narrows until it becomes little more than a canyon. About 5 miles after starting we came to some Indian ranches with large, well cultivated fields of wheat and oats. Occasionally we crossed a sparkling stream flowing down from the mountain; if utilized these streams would irrigate a large part of the slope lying between the talus of the mountain and the river.

At the Indian ranches just mentioned a courier, in great haste, overtook us, seeking for medical assistance for a miner, who the day before had been seriously injured by a blast. The distance was some 30 miles back and too great to send assistance but Dr. Moore explained to the messenger the course of treatment to pursue with the wounded man.

Most of the trail today was exceedingly rough, leading over great piles of rock that had slid and rolled down from the mountains. At one place the trail had been washed away by a recent cloud burst, and we had to get around the break by going up over and exceedingly rough side of the mountain.

We encamped on the bank of the river a few hundred yards below the mouth of Graveyard Creek the river is full of trout and white fish, great numbers of which were caught by the fishermen of our party.

A short distance from our encampment was another party, consisting of an English gentleman and his wife, and two or three children. They had a comfortable outfit of pack animals, and were on their way from Hope to the Okinakane. The Okinakane country has great reputation with the people of British Columbia for its productiveness and the salubrity of its climate, great indeed should be these advantages to counterbalance the difficulties to be overcome in reaching that remote region, and stout of hearts must be the woman, who with her children undertakes the journey. Children are carried over these rough trails on horse or mules, held on by an Indian riding the same animal. There was little or no grass at our camp of this evening.

August 16 - During the night we had a slight thunder shower, the first rain we have had since leaving the park. We are glad to have it, hoping that it will clear the atmosphere of smoke, and give us a better opportunity of seeing the splendid scenery through which we are traveling.

The morning opened clear, but as we were mounting to start it commenced again to shower, and kept up for an hour. Soon after crossing the Graveyard Creek the trail took the side of the mountain and was exceedingly rough, crooked, and sidling. Graveyard Creek is so named from a small Indian burial place near its mouth. The graveyard is enclosed with a fence, and ornamented with rude carvings.

About 6 miles from this creek we came to Allison ranch. This place was formerly known as Princeton, the name of gold mines in the vicinity. These mines are no longer worked, but the remains of old ditches are still to be seen winding around the hills through the forest. Allison's place consists of a comfortable log dwelling, and a few outbuildings. In one of the latter is kept a small store, or what might flatteringly be called a store; who the customers are difficult to tell. Allison himself was absent, being at Victoria, but his courteous wife received us with hospitality. She is a rosy-cheeked English woman, apparently about twenty-five, but is old enough to boast of ten children, healthy, handsome urchins, another instance, as before remarked, that the more distant and difficult of access the place, the more prolific are the human inhabitants. She informed us that she had been residing here fifteen years. She appeared cheerful, happy, and contented, in her isolated home.

Allison's business here is cattle raising, and although there is no grass, nor signs of grass anywhere about his ranch, it is said there is good grazing in the foot hills not far off. The cattle are driven to the valley of the Okinakane for wintering; there hay is put up for that purpose. The distance to the Okinakane is about 50 miles. The cattle finally find their way across the boundary into Washington Territory at the Osoyoos custom house, and from thence eastward to a market. They start as yearlings and come out full grown beeves. Allison's ranch is about a mile below the junction of the west and south forks of the Similkameen.

Crossing the West Fort at a ford very rough with boulders, we soon commenced to ascent to a rolling table land covered with heavy timber ad well clothed with grass-- fine and bunch grass mixed. The ascent to this plateau was over a difficult trail, as was likewise the decent.

On the way we passed first Five, and then Nine-mile Creeks; the distances being taken from Allison after leaving the plateau the trail was very much broken by small tributaries of the Whipsaw Creek. The latter creek follows in this part of its course a deep canyon, along raged edge of which the trail winds far above the dashing stream.

I'll have to stop it here. Within the next two days they were in Fort Hope and camping along the Fraser River. I hope you like this brief encounter with Civil War History and how it connects with our Okanogan Country.

Pictographs in Okanogan Country
ANM

There are many of these kinds of pictographs in the area and the Okanogan People would appreciate it if you would not destroy any that you find.   The Okanogan Nation Alliance, the Okanagan Indian People, and the Members of the Confederated Tribes of the Colville Reservation hold these pictographs as sacred sign of our People and their tradition, custom and culture.

Marked Trees   ANM

These are pictures of images in trees that have no rhyme or reason. The university group that came to study them was completely baffled.

There were many more trees with this marking on them, at that time, and now there are but a few left standing. Some are still recognizable on the ground, but are deteriorating rapidly. They are in the San Poil valley on the Colville Reservation.

San Poil Madonna ANM

This is a picture of the San Poil Madonna. During a time of great suffering the People prayed for help and when she appeared, the sickness was relieved and the suffering of the People taken away.

There are a few People left that can tell the whole story of the San Poil Madonna that live near Keller on the Colville Reservation. They are among the elders of our People and their names cannot be given out in this text. They are a rich and valuable asset to our People and their gift of history, tradition, custom and culture should not be ignored.

Coyote Rock ANM

This is a picture of the Coyote (Sinklip); it is located in the canyon between Omak and Nespelem near the summit. The Coyote stands watch and for a very good reason.

The story was told to Virgil "Smoker" Marchand in the late summer of 1993 by Ms Alice Irey and was told to her by her uncle. Ms Alice Irey is a very good and kind person with a big smile to greet everyone. She is the epitome of what an elder should be and how they give to their People.

His story is about the area we know as Coyote Canyon and the locals used to call it Refrigerator

Canyon. Coyote can be seen to point 1 miles south of Disautel Summit looking across the canyon. **"The Way I Heard It":**

"Coyote & his wife Gopher"

Coyote and his wife, Gopher, were coming from the Okanogan River and heading for the Columbia River. They were following the Salmon which used to come through the canyon following the water that flowed through the canyon.

Drawing byArnie Marchand

Coyote and his wife, Gopher, got into an argument; he often argued with her. Coyote got really mad at Gopher, because when they would fight, she would go underground and he could not follow her. So, this time when she went underground he turned the flow of the water passing through the canyon underground! This would flood her out! She got away underground.

Now, you can see that the water no longer flows through the canyon. But it flows underground starting from Coyote Creek Campground and comes out at the ponds just beyond the canyon on Highway #155.

Coyote is still there watching and waiting for Gopher to come out from under ground.

Spotted Lake ANM

This is a picture of a very sacred medicine lake called "Spotted Lake" just a few miles from Osoyoos, B.C. west on highway #3.

Spotted Lake was returned to the Okanagan Nation in 2001. The Federal Government purchased the land from private ownership with negotiations by Chief Clarence Louie, of the Osoyoos Indian Band and Chief Dan Wilson, of the Okanagan Indian Band.

I know both of these men and they are of exemplar dedication to their People and Indian Country.

Spotted Lake is the central point of the Okanagan. This lake is a chief among lakes where all water, minerals, and salt converge.

Our People view the lake as many lakes within a lake. It has been a sacred place to us from time immemorial. Spotted Lake is comprised of 365 circles of various shapes and depths. Each circle contains a particular healing quality. Our People have used each circle as a separate medicine when we are sick or in need of spiritual inspiration. We go down to the lake and use its power. Anyone who goes to the lake will find the right circles if he or she seeks its power.

There was a celebration of the return of the lake to us, and many of our People came. I brought my youngest son, Josh and he, for the first time in his young life, experienced something he will be able to tell his grandchildren. It was a very spiritual and moving day for all of those who were at the celebration of Spotted Lake.

It is an example of the rich history and culture that is in Indian Country and one only has to take the time to do a little research and ask local historical museums such as the Wenatchee Valley Museum and Cultural Center, Chelan Historical Society, Okanogan County Historical Society, the Colville Tribal Museum, the Lake Chelan Historical Society, Okanogan Borderland Historical Society, the En'owkin Centre in Penticton, B.C., and libraries. There is an organization that numbers more than thirty members called the Upper Columbia Museum Association where you can get you a good start on the region and its rich and colorful history.

Before the European arrived, the Okanagan Nation had to defend its land and People, and remember the story of "Namtu'stem", or McIntyre Bluff.

McIntyre Bluff   ANM

"The Way I Heard It":

A Shu Shwap raiding party came down to the Okanagan. They camped on the top of McIntyre Bluff the night before the raid. The Okanagan surrounded the back of the bluff and the battle began.

The Shu Shwap had to either fight and die or plunge off the cliffs at McIntyre Bluff. In the end, the battle favored the Okanagan. Only a few were left, one was a "shaman" and was allowed to return home to tell of their tragic defeat.

Another version of the story that I heard goes like this:

The Shu Shwap crept into Okanogan Country and camped by McIntyre Bluff at night to surprise the Okanagan in the morning.

The Okanagan were ready and when they made camp the Okanagan made fires of the hill opposite the bluff and let the   Shu Shwap think we were unaware of their presence. Just before dawn the Okanagan began the attack. The Shu Shwap were surprised begun to fight and retreat at the same time. Unaware of the cliffs they fought and ran, fought and ran, always toward the camp fires of their enemies. Coming to the cliffs they plunged off and all died.

There was one or two left, the "shaman" who was blind and a couple others. The shaman moved among the battle untouched, because we are never to bother the handicapped, for they have been touched by God. The shaman moved with a staff during the battle and found that there was a cliff, he stopped. At the end of the battle he and a couple of helpers were allowed to return and tell of their defeat. As they journeyed back the way they came, they passed White Lake, where one of the helpers drowned.

Skaha Lake ANM

Skaha Lake had name like "Dog Lake" and Okanagan Falls had a name like "Dog Town".

Then, the ladies of the day thought it would be more appealing to call it Skaha Lake and Okanagan Falls. That is from the brochure of the town.

Actually, 'Dog Lake' is from a Shu Shwap Indian word, "Skaha" not an Okanogan Indian word. The native, First Nations People here were Okanagan Indians, not Shu Shwap. A story I heard a long time ago was that an epidemic was going through this area and we prayed for help and a sign from above was the appearance of a horseman on the cliff.

Near Vaseux Lake near Okanagan Falls, BC, is a picture of a horse and rider and a coyote behind the horse. When I was a kid I saw the picture from the road and it was vivid and black and easy to see. My parents did not tell me the story of the picture on the cliff, but they said there was one and they didn't listen when the story was told.

I have watched the picture on the cliff slowly fade from sight and this is the clearest one I have, and it's bad. I've often wondered about the story, but I've found no one to date that can remember it.

Cliff Face ANM

The area near the radio communication facility is an area my mother said they used to come to when she was a child. Her mother and she would spend weeks near White Lake gathering roots and berries for the winter. She said her memory was a "fond" and quiet time and she enjoy telling some stories, but mostly remembering.

When you start around the road keep looking at the cliff face to the south. Quickly it will turn into the face of a man, and then suddenly disappear!

There is a story about something that happened near here. I think it was near Green Lake. When

Mom said it went something like this: so this is
"The Way I Heard It":

A young man was riding in the area, on a hill side
and was working some cows of a local rancher.
He began to hear noises from a distance and he
began to get curious. He could hear faint almost
quiet laughter! Like a kid would make, a young
kid. But why, where, how could a kid be way out
here without their parents, and there is no sign of
anybody in miles of this place. It has steep hills,
rocky ground, and one lake, hard to get too; no
way could a wagon get up here.

Yet there it is again, that laughter! As he walked
his horse down the hill a bit farther and he could
hear the laughter better, but still...... He got off his
horse and walked down the hillside a little farther
and there it was......wait, what is that? It looks
like a little kid, with yellow hair and funny
colored? The kid was laughing. The cowboy
stood frozen in his tracks. He looked and watched
the kid play in the water a while. Then it was as
though the kid knew he was there, and taunted the
cowboy to come down to the water.

The cowboy reluctantly moved closer. The
playfulness of the kid seemed harmless enough,
and the cowboy came closer to get a better look. It

was a kid! And it was swimming out to the middle and back and then just to get still in the water and wait.

The cowboy watched and thought the kid was waving him into the lake. The cowboy stood up and really took a look at the kid. Then as suddenly as it appeared, it waved turned slowly over and disappeared. The laughter was gone. Where did the kid go? The cowboy thought a long time on this and on his way home thought who could he tell such a story too?

After a time, the cowboy finally told his grandpa, and grandpa said something like this:

There are Little People in our world that if you get curious enough and close enough, they can take you. No one knows where they take you, but you will never return. You are lucky. If you ever get in that situation again, don't let your curiosity get ahold of you, think about who you are and what you are doing, and leave!

Okanogan Lake ANM

This is the place called the house of the Ogapoga. There are many stories of the Ogapoga and the museums and libraries have all you can read of them.

I was told a story and was asked never to tell anyone that he told this story. It was in the late summer and they were going down to Okanagan Lake from their house. They were walking through the woods near the lake and could see the lake and were getting very close to the shore.

His mother felt it first rather than seeing something, and then in the woods near the shore there it was!!

Moving in a meandering slow movement in the shallow water of the lake; they stopped and watched it for what seemed like an eternity, but was probably only five minutes or so. Then, as quickly as it appeared it moved quickly to deeper water and disappeared.

Both never told anyone but very close family, because of the ridicule the non-Indian community had for Natives at that time and this would not help with anything. The one who told me this story was with his mother and he was a grown man at the time. His mother has passed now, but if she said it no one would ever dispute her. Both people are very well respected and I will never reveal their names.

Horses by Okanagan Lake   ANM

My Father told me of an event he went through and he made me swear not to tell anyone probably because of that same attitude they all had to live with in those times.

You see if you spoke of such a thing, you would be laughed at and thought to be kind of "not all there".

My Dad was a very proud man and would not take such treatment, so he and his uncle and cousin never spoke of it again.

He never told the story to anyone, except my Mom. I tried to get him to tell me, but he wouldn't for a lot of reasons. I argued with him a lot to tell me stories of his past and it took my Mom to get him to tell this one. She said something to him in Okanagan and that's all it took. And **"The Way I Heard It"**:

"We, my uncle and my cousin and I were traveling south along the lake from Six Mile (creek) working a few cows toward a ranch we were to bring them to in the morning. The weather was bad and not very far along the way it started to rain, then it really began to rain like "in buckets"! We were all drenched and had to find shelter quickly.

We saw an old log cabin unoccupied and put the horses under the trees and went inside. It was late afternoon and the weather was not going to let up today or tonight. We made a fire, ate a little and waited for the rain to subside so we could continue our journey. It was really late and we bedded down for the night.

About one or two in the morning we were awakened by a noise that sounded like a freight train coming right through the cabin. It was loud and we had never heard such a sound, or such a sound so loud, during any storm! It seemed to be coming from the hill behind the cabin. Then it came closer and closer, and we all thought it could be a washout or something. The noise never stopped and the horses were going crazy! The sound was really loud and it came by the cabin and then seemed to fade south of us into the rain storm.

The horses settled down and in the morning we were up by dawn, and the storm had passed. It was cool and we looked for what made that noise.

We circled the cabin and found a trench, yes a trench a few feet deep and it came right down the hill behind the cabin, turned south and proceeded south along what is now a road and then down to the lake. It scared us and we never told of this to anyone and the local ranchers that saw the new trench only figured it was a peculiar wash out."

I ask my Dad, "Why didn't you go up the mountain to see where it came from?" He looked at me like I was crazy! Mom asked him why and he told her, in Indian, that he was scared and never thought of investigating that thing that made that deep trench and disappeared into Okanagan Lake.

The cave high up in the mountain behind that old cabin has been logged over, the road along the lake is now a paved road, and cabin has since fell down and disappeared. But every time I pass by that sight I can still see a vague reference to the trench and remember the story. This was one of the only times I can remember my Dad ever being scared of anything.

My Dad told me very little about such stories and refused to teach me my language. It is not uncommon among the People of his era. They were told, threatened, and sometimes sent away to keep the language from being learned, remembered or taught. The government called it "assimilation", a way to strip you of your language, custom, culture and religion.

My Dad once told me, "I will teach you your language when the day comes that someone will pay you to talk it!" I knew that day would never come. My Dad and Mom lived and worked in a society that did not tolerate anyone speaking anything but English. Even though they knew the people demanding English were only a generation or so away from their parents or grandparents growing up on a foreign language in a foreign country.

Dad and Mom did see the time that Indians were paid to teach Indian to Indians. It happened on the Colville Reservation in 1990. The Tribal Planning Department received a grant to initiate a language program on the Reservation. The languages Nsyilxcn, Nxaʔamcxi'n, and Nimipu are now taught in five school districts and two community colleges and one four year college.

My Dad and Mom were amazed to hear of such a thing when their whole life was to live in the shadow of a people that treated us (Indian People) much like third class citizens. Today it is not like that world at all, and it is always improving.

"The Trek" ANM

Another story about the Ogapoga was related to me by paddlers on the first Canoe TREK from Pillar Rock, the northern most part of our country near Enderby, B.C. down the many lakes to the mouth of the Okanogan River. The trip was accompanied by a group of horsemen riding the route in 2001.

It was the first time our People traversed our territory in a traditional manner in more than 150 years.

It began with a dream that came to an extremely honorable elder named Mrs. Louise Gabriel of the Penticton Indian Band.

The dream was of her lying on shore and watching the People go by on the lake in canoes.

194

She said she couldn't recognize them, they seemed to be either not looking at her or going too fast or she just couldn't see them clearly enough. She kept the dream to herself and then told some of her family and then to the Elders Council. They helped translate the dream.

Canoes on the Osoyoos Lake ANM

It was decided to ride the entire length of our territory to reclaim and reinvigorate our youth to our traditions, custom and culture. It was a great undertaking, first who do we know that can remember or make a canoe. That responsibility fell to Gordon Marchand of the Head of the Lake Band of the Okanagan. He knew how to make traditional canoes and he would teach the youth and all of the bands how to build them. Each of the seven Bands of the Okanagan set out to accomplish this task.

They used cottonwood trees and made their own tools to see how difficult it was to do it the old ways. They, of course, used modern tools very extensively throughout the project. They built many canoes and the youth, women and men were all represented by a canoe built by each group or band. The women's canoe was the best built and built by only women and rowed by only women, even an elder or two. The distinction of the women's canoe was that their canoe never tipped over once during the entire TREK and it was the most notable. The canoe that carried the "staff" was the honor canoe.

These canoes can be seen at each of the bands and often in parades and lectures.

But back to the story, the canoes were coming up along (near) the Ogapoga' House on Okanagan Lake. There were very large wide waves and somewhat of a wind on the lake and the paddling was difficult. The waves were so high that the canoe could disappear behind one and often did. During one of those descents into the bottom of the wave, a large dark "Thing" slithered by "in" one of those waves. The lead rower and rear rower both saw the thing and looked in awe of such an event happening on the TREK.

They never said anything right away and told only a few of us later of the happening. It was as if (he) the Ogapoga was giving his blessing to the event and looking at us at the same time. When I was told of the happening it made the hair stand up on my neck.

Sophie Verdon Marchand ANM

This is a picture of my Mother, and a child. It's only a picture until you hear the story. She said she was at a rodeo in Penticton, B.C., about 1932 or before.

A photographer and his wife were roaming around taking pictures and paying people to pose for them.

When they asked Mom, she wondered why anyone would want a picture of her? They said, "Do you have a baby?" Mom said, "No." "Can you get a baby?" So mom went over to her aunt and asked her for the child. A friend gave her a purse and she went back to the cart she was standing beside earlier.

She asked them why they didn't take a picture of the bear just on the other side of the cart. She told them that it was her bear and it does tricks, and that she had it in the parade earlier and it was very entertaining. They seemed more interested in her and offer a few coins to take the picture. She took the picture and they left thanking her on the way.

The two photographers came upon a small man squatting by the fence and facing away from the rodeo. He was dressed in a canvas kind of pants roughly sewn together down both sides and a similar shirt with a slit opening for his head to go through. The canvas was old and dirty and he smelled very "ripe" for that time of day.

The photographer asked "Who are you!" and the answer was "I'm chief!" the photographer asked if he could take the picture of him being he was chief! He said "No!" The photographer said, "I'll give you $5", and the little man nodded his head vigorously in the affirmative and the picture was taken.

A few months had gone by and Mom had to travel to town (Penticton) to get a few things from the drug store and other places. She took her father's wagon and went to town. She did a few errands and arrived at the drug store. She had to wait back near the door until the local customers were taken care of by the druggist. While waiting she noticed a greeting card rack and started to look at the pictures.

And "What do you know" there she was in her regalia, baby and all! And next to it a picture of a little Chinese man with a shabby goatee, balding head of not much gray hair and a very dirty canvas outfit held up with an old rope. Under that picture was the name "Indian Chief" and under her picture post card was "Indian Princess with child."

She went up to the druggist and asked about the pictures, they were selling for five cents. The druggist said that photographer and his wife had come to him and many other business people and sold them from Vancouver to where ever, that he had 10,000 of them.

Mom couldn't do anything about the whole matter and told me the story when we came upon the picture some years later. I went into the Penticton Museum and saw the same picture at the entrance, a five foot cutout of mom holding the baby.

I asked the manager for the cutout after they were finished with it. The manager respectfully declined and months later I tried again and he said it either got lost or someone lost it. Strange isn't it?

Massacre of Indians

Peter Grauer, the author of <u>"Interred with their Bones, Bill Miner in Canada" 1903 to 1907.</u>" introduced me to this story that tells of a firsthand account of a massacre of Okanagan Indians. It was written by Herman Francis Reinhart, and edited by Joyce B. Nunis Jr. under the title "The Golden Frontier".

The book is a recollection of the authors travels up from the Yakima Country into the Okanagan Valley and on to the gold fields and the Frazer River in B.C.

The book is very interesting and is a first hand account of a trip throughout the old west from Wyoming to California to the Frazer River country. Starting on page #119 it goes like this:

"Our major and advance guard would pick our camping places. We had a fearful bad road or trail-no road, just an Indian trail, over rocks, hills, mountains and streams both wide and deep and cold. Many of us had to walk, and all in a hurry to get to Fraser River.

We were loaded too heavy, and drove too fast for our stock, and every day some ponies would give out and be left. Some would kill them, but mostly would just leave them to graze and shift for themselves. I had to leave my roan mare that I had traded by S.M. Charles pistol for eight or nine days from Fort Simcoe. I had to put the most of his load on the other horse, and some on Bill Cochran's.

In a few days my bay horse commenced weakening with the heavy load, and I had to get a packer to take a hundred pounds of flour for me. Bill Cochran's commenced weakening and we took our only riding horse and put part of the load on him. Every day horses and mules gave out, until forty or fifty men would have to walk, or change with each other, half the time, riding.

Then we had many long stretches without water, road were rocky and again so dusty, 700 horse and mules passing along raised an awful dust, and us forty men had to walk fast behind each other's mules and horses, that sometimes we were nearly choked with dust and drought.

Our boots would hurt our feet, and some of us would have to walk in socks or rags, or make carpet-shoes to keep the rocks and prickly pears from our feet. Some of us suffered awful, but there was no stopping, we had to keep up with each other or be left behind in a dangerous Indian country, where were watching us to cut us off from each other, or attack us every opportunity.

I never suffered so much in my life as on that trip to Fraser River. My ankles are naturally weak, and I would sprain them every little while; they would swell up so that I could hardly get along, but I had to drag on anyway. I made me moccasins of carpet from a saddlecloth I had, and I would have to put on a new sole every night after I got into camp.

How glad many of us were when we stopped to something at the crossing of some stream, or to water all our stock at some lake, so that we could sit down and rest our sore feet. But the different companies some wanted to go faster, others slower. Some would get up earlier and be ready to start sooner that other, and such a confusion and wrangle I never saw! Some would threaten to go on, and accuse each other of cowardice and fear of Indians.

The old Californian miners and Indian-fighters were the worst; they claimed they could travel in small parties and clean out all the Indians in the land, and others were all cowards, and it was all our major and captains could do to control their men, to stay together, for if we had scattered out and separated from each other, the Indians would have completely annihilated us all, and all men of reason know it.

Drawing by Arnie Marchand

When we got to a small stream emptying into the Columbia River, called the Weewich, a good many miners wished to lay by a couple of weeks to prospect the stream and its gulches, for some gold had been found, good prospects; but the majority wanted to go on. It was left to a vote and was carried to go on and not to prospect till we got to Thompson River or Lake. We got to Lake Chelan and had to construct rafts for ourselves and goods and swim horses and mules over the river and lake.

One morning we had camped within a mile or two of a large stream that ran into the Columbia 10 or 12 miles below the mouth of the Okanogan River and Fort Okanogan. Some of the miners had lost sight of their horses, and before they had got them packed up the head of the train started on. Either they did not know that many were not ready or they did not care.

William Cochran's horse was one of the lost but we found him sooner than some others did theirs, and we loaded up and started to catch up to our company, just crossing the stream or river. Will and I had to get on our packs on the horses to cross. The water was very cold and waist deep. Our horses were very weak and our weights on them made them more so.

So we had a hard time in crossing to the other side. Then we got off and straightened our packs.

Men were passing and re-passing, belonging to our command. I could still see some pack trains who had not finished loading, and some getting up their animals, so we pushed on slowly. My bay horse was nearly given out, and awful weak. I expected every hour to have to leave him. Our train was scattered for two or three miles along the bottom, on the side of the Columbia River. We could see the advance guard way ahead, over three miles.

The bar next the river was narrow, with a high mountain on our left. We were on the bank of the creek we had just crossed and had started out three head of horses ahead of us, driving them in the trail, when all at once we heard some shooting across the creek we had just crossed.

We stopped and looked back and saw four horsemen coming out of the stream, running their horses hard as they could go. We thought they were racing, and Will and I both stopped and rested on our guns to see who would beat. As they came closer I saw *they were two Mexicans and two Frenchmen, and they were shouting "Indians! Indians!" and had their pistols in their hands and spurring their horse at their best speed. When near they called to us to run, that the Indians were killing some Frenchmen and Mexicans right behind us. They tried to help us drive our horses, but my bay, nearly-give-out horse, turned to one side and Will Cochran's turned to the other side of the trail, and the third kept along the trail. So the Mexicans and Frenchmen told us to leave the horses and run head, and they went on and left us, and run their horses by our jaded animals.*

So I called to Bill Cochran to get on his best horse and start on ahead in the trail and I would drive the two others, for they would be apt to follow better. He done so, and I put a fresh cap on my rifle and thinks "I cannot get away anyway if the Indians are a horseback," so I drove as fast as my poor old bay horse could go, in a slow walk.

Now all the money and gold specimens and my $24 ring and my fine double breast-pin were in a sack with some clothing of mine, and it was made fast with a rope with *a sack of flour and a five gallon keg of East Boston syrup. I could not take time to take the sack of clothes and my money out off the horse in the excitement. So I told Bill Cochran I would stay with the bay horse, for if I left him I would be broke anyway. I made up my mind to stay and fight it out and not try and run and leave everything I had in the world. Just then two or three shots were fired behind me, and the bay horse struck a trot for about fifty yards and weakened again.*

I expected every minute the next shot would strike me, but we kept on and the first thing we saw, our Maj. Robinson and some of the advanced guard coming back toward us, not very fast but badly frightened. And they asked us where the Indians ere I told them to hurry back and go faster or they would not see any, and they clapped spurs to their horses, and some whipped them, and back they went until eighty or a hundred men had gone back.

They kept on and found our train scattered for five miles along the Columbia River...If there had been forty or fifty determined Indians, they could have commenced behind and killed half of our whole command whilst they were running to get on the next bar of the river to draw up in shape to fight. I never saw so many men so well armed and able to fight any amount of Indians, had they been rightly handled, and not so panic-stricken.

Some laughable incidents took place; some of the French company jumped on their pack horses and rushed them by each other running over one another and knocking down all in their way. One old California miner named Pike was so excited that he said he saw at least fifteen hundred Indians on the side of the mountains ready to attack us. When we got up to where our company was, we stopped and waited to hear from the rear. As yet no news had been brought forward, but by the four men that gave the alarm.

After a while some of our men came back where we were ready to stand and attack if the Indians should defeat our Major and what men had gone back. And soon they returned with one dead man of Company B. Now I will relate the circumstances.

There was a French blacksmith in the French company; and he had some nine or ten mules loaded with goods for a general store such as groceries, boots and shoes, clothing, a set of blacksmith tools all for himself; he had bellows, anvil and vise, and iron and steel. He was from Yreka, California and had an old Mexican man helping him to pack his mules.

Another Frenchman in the same company wanted to buy a pair of boots from him on time, or when he could get work, when he would get to Fraser River and make money to pay him for them. He was nearly barefooted.

But the blacksmith refused to let him have them...the French in his company did not like the blacksmith because he had plenty of means and was too close or mean for them. That morning the blacksmith's mules were hard to find, and it was late when he did find them, so that the French company got ready and just left him long before he got ready, for none would help him to load.

So he and the old Mexican were working as hard as possible to get loaded and catch up to the balance of the train. They were way behind when they all got loaded. They noticed some eight or nine Indians on horseback coming toward them. There were some four or five Mexicans and French just starting out, and had got a few hundred yards from camp when they heard some firing of guns, and looking back, saw the Indians, shooting at the old Mexican and blacksmith and driving off their pack animals.

But the four or five Mexicans and French, instead of going to help the blacksmith and old Mexican, came on after the train and to those ahead, with the result already stated.

Now if the four horsemen and one or two close by had gone back and helped the blacksmith and his Mexican (they all had big revolvers and two or three rifles or shotguns), they could have whipped or drove off the Indians, there being only eight or nine in number. But they got frightened and thought there was a large body of Indians, got excited and left them to give the alarm and get out of danger themselves. Or if they had told us, we both had rifles and revolvers, and altogether we would have been about the number of the Indians.

But the Old Mexican, when shot, fell as if dead, and crawled off into the brush. The blacksmith had run off, the Indians shooting at him as he ran. Two or three Indians rode on after a white foot man right ahead, and not over sixty yards behind me, and killed him. And then turned back and with the other Indians drove off the blacksmith's nine pack mules and his one riding mule, and on the saddle of the riding mule a pair of leather cantinas containing $700 in cold coins, and revolver and a shotgun hanging to the riding saddle.

The Indians just rushed the mules up the mountains, two of them too heavy loaded to drive fast, had on the anvil, bellows and some iron. They just cut the ropes and cut the packs loose, and drove the mules right along with the others, and by the time the Major and our men got back where they had been, they were three or four miles up in the mountains, and the Major and men were afraid to follow for fear there might be an Indian ambush. So they let them go without a struggle, for Maj. Robinson's former bad luck did not encourage him to take the chances of being drawn into fight on the *mountains and maybe ambushed, and the balance of the train five miles off, and maybe watched by thousands of Indians. At least he was being cautious after the blunder of the morning.*

The French blacksmith came out of his hiding place to where our men was, and told them that the old Mexican was shot dead not far off, that he saw him fall. But just then the old man came out of the brush where he had been hiding unhurt.

That man killed behind me belonged to Company B and had lost a horse and had been out across the stream, and Bill Cochran and I met him in the stream on his way back to camp.

He told us of losing his horse (we were on the tops of our packs to keep from getting wet and cold); when he saw the Indians attack the blacksmith and come running after us. The two or three Indians saw him alone and that he had a pistol with him and came after him on horseback and shot him with their rifles; even after he lay on his face they shot him in the head. It was their shots we heard so close by that made my bay horse trot, they being but about sixty yards behind me.

But there was a ridge between me and them and they did not see us two, nor we them, or if they seen us, saw that we both had rifles, and it might not have paid them to take equal chances with us.

Now the strangest part of the whole thing was that the man killed had his horse taken and no other; I thought it strange and it came to my mind. He was a teamster at The Dalles, and Irishman named McCandless; he joined at Fort Simcoe. One evening two or three days out from Simcoe an old Indian was caught prowling around our camp and stock, looking among the horses. He was arrested by the guard and brought to the Major's headquarters to see what should be done with him.

The Irishman killed was very loudly in favor of shooting the Indian as a spy and was very persistent in trying to influence other miners to have him shot, and every Indian we should meet, friendly or hostile. The Indian understood the Irishman's threats (what he was in favor of and he would do). The Indian said he was a

215

friendly, peaceable Indian, a Yakima, and did not mean any harm in coming to our camp, that some of his horses had been drove off by some Indians horse thief and taken to The Dalles, and he thought he knew the horse McCandless had was his horse, but by a vote the Indian was told to go and not be seen again or he would be shot.

And McCandless, the Irishman, told the Indian he had a good notion to shoot him. My surmise is that the Indian and his friends followed us for an opportunity to steal horses or to kill a lot of us, but could not get a good chance until then. They knew his horse and took it, knowing he would have to hunt it, and they could maybe kill him, which they did by chance by there being no rear guard that morning.... We knew we were close to Fort Okanogan...and thought there would be no danger of Indians, although we knew we were watched and followed all the way from Fort Simcoe.

We camped on the bar and dug a grave close to the bank of the Columbia River and buried McCandless. No one knew anything about him, only that he had drove teams for the government at The Dalles. He may have been in the first Robinson Company when drove back by the Indians two months before it may have made him bitterer toward the Indians and made him wish to kill them whenever he could for revenge. So it ended.

Next morning about ten o'clock we got to Fort Okanogan, an old Hudson Bay trading post. A few half breeds and a couple of Frenchmen with Indian wives kept the place, and plenty of Indians (they said they were friendly) around. They did not seem to know of the attack on our train and of the killing of the man. I think they did know, and maybe had a hand in it. If we had had any proof of it, we would soon have taken and burnt up the old fort and killed every one of them—our men were just in the humor for it.

We had not gone but a few miles until my bay horse gave out, so I had to leave him. So my two horses had been left within ten or twelve days out from Fort Simcoe.

We crossed the Okanogan River close to a high rocky pass canyon and some of our men made remarks that some large body of men and horse had been running and tramping around—signs of Indians on the hills and the men thought what a place it would be for the Indians to attack us, or so surround and ambush us in the canyon which we had to pass through. Twenty-five well armed men among the rocks could have defeated our whole train, being away up among the rocks which they could have rolled down on us and stampeded our horses and mules.

We felt a little squeamish when some of our men found a place where there were four or five new made graves. On a headboard it says:

Captain David McLaughlin and 157 men passed on the 27th of June, 1858, and in an Indian attack and fight at the crossing of the river and canyon five of their men were killed and the company had to back out of the canyon and cross back over the river and go around this pass or canyon. The Indians had defeated them, killing 28 or 30 horses. But we got through all right, without trouble, and we had a guard of men on the top of the highest rocks in the canyon to keep any Indian from attempting to molest us.

I knew Dave McLaughlin. He was a half breed son of old Dr. McLaughlin of Oregon City.

The old doctor had been superintendent of the Hudson Bay Fur Company; he was very rich and Capt. Dave was his only son. He was considered a fast young man to drink, gamble and carouse, and a great Indian fighter and scout in several Indian wars on the pacific coast.

His company left The Dalles ahead of Maj. Robinson first company, but they kept up the Columbia on the east side up to Fort Walla Walla, then on to Spokane and crossed the Columbia River just below Fort Okanogan, and here was our first news of him or his company.

For a few days we traveled along with great care, constantly on the lookout for an Indian attack. We crossed several nice streams and fine looking farming and grazing land, and got to the British line. Here about a hundred Californians out of our train concluded to go a different route, by way of the Similkameen, then on to Fort Hope, down low on the Fraser River.

We tried to talk them out of going that way, but no, they were not afraid of Indians, and could travel where they wished to for all the Indians in British America. There were mostly from Northern California (I will speak of this command further on).

In a few days we got to Okanogan Lake. Our advance guards saw some Indians just leaving their camp across the lake in canoes for fear of us. The boys saw a couple of their dogs at their old camp ground and shot them down, and they saw some old huts where the Indians had stored a lot of berries for the winter, blackberries and nuts, fifty or a hundred bushels. They helped themselves to the berries and nuts, filling several sacks to take along, and the balance they just emptied into the lake, destroying them so that the Indians wouldn't have them for provisions for winter. I, and a great many others, expressed their opinion that it was very imprudent and uncalled for, and no doubt the Indians would retaliate.

But they only laughed and thought it great fun to kill their dogs and destroy and rob them of their provisions. Most everyone but those who had done it disapproved of the whole affair.

The next night we camped on the bank of Lake Okanogan, which is about 150 miles long and from one to six miles wide. Next morning a man named White, of Company B, could not find his horse. Some of his friends helped hunt for it, but as the train went on the men were coming down the hill, and someone fired a shot at White, and some men above his on the hill saw some Indians trying to cut White off from his companions. The men called to White to go down as the Indians were after him. So they gave up the horse, and did not look anymore, for the train had already started on.

We traveled along the lake all day and camped on the banks at night. Every morning after we left camp some Indians would come across the lake in canoes and look over our camp grounds to look if we had left or thrown away anything (sometimes we threw away old clothes, hats, shoes, shirts or old blankets or crusts of bread or meat, and they come and get them after we left.....That morning the advance guard planned to punish the Indians if they should come to camp as usual after we left.

So right after breakfast some 25 men concealed themselves in a gulch close to camp, and the train went on as usual. We were passing along a high trail close to the lake and we so saw three or four canoes start to come across from the other side, with seven or eight Indians in each canoe, to go to our camping place. I had gone with the train, some one and a fourth to one and one half miles, when we heard some shooting. I stopped to listen and counted over fifty shots.

In the course of half an hour our advance guard that had formed the ambush came up to us and related how they were all lying down in the gulch, to be out of sight, and they got to talking to each other and forgot about the Indians to be ambushed, and they were surprised as well as the Indians, for the Indians had landed and were coming towards the camp right to where the white men lay concealed.

They had no idea of danger from the whites, so some whites happened to rise up to see if the Indians had landed yet, when behold! The Indian were within eight or ten feet from him, and they did not see the whites till they all raised and made a rush for the Indians with their guns and pistols all ready to shoot.

As soon as the Indians saw the whites, they were so frightened that some turned back and ran towards their boats; some fell down on their knees and begged for them not to shoot, as they had no arms at all, and they threw up their hands and arms to show that they had nothing.

But the whites all commenced to fire and shoot at them, and ran out to the lake after those who were getting in their canoes, and kept on shooting till the few that got into the canoes got out of reach of their guns and rifles. And lots jumped into the lake and were shot in the water before they could swim out of reach of their murderers— for it was a great slaughter or massacre of Indians killed, for they never made an effort to resist or fired a shot, either gun, pistol, or bow and arrows, and the men were not touched, no more than if they had shot at birds or fish.

It was a brutal affair, but the perpetrators of the outrage thought they were heroes and were victors in some well fought battle. The Indians were completely dumbfounded to see a lot of armed men when they expected no one, and ran toward their canoes to get away, and the Indians knelt down and begged for life saying they were friends. There must have been 10 or 12 killed and that many wounded for every few got away unhurt. Some must have got drowned and as I said before, it was like killing chickens or dogs or hogs, and a deed Californians should ever be ashamed of, without counting the after-consequence."

This account of the massacre was typical of the type of travelers of the Caribou Trail. There were many accounts of "skirmishes with local Indians" in many historical records and that is how they were portrayed in history as "Skirmishes".

Now you have heard of a firsthand account of a skirmish that occurred along the Okanogan Lake. It gives one some thought as to what actually happened and what was actually written in the days of the Caribou Trail.

Lake Okanogan close to Westbank ANM

This is a story I finally got my Dad to tell me just before he passed. It was hard to get him to tell anything about himself. This is **"The Way I Heard It"**:

Dad said he and his friend were riding horseback near Westbank and they went up a draw that had a small creek.

"We went up the draw a ways and then turned back up the hill behind a cottonwood grove. It was cool and it was summer, so we decided to rest and look around, maybe have lunch. They left the horses and wandered through the grove of trees and walked into a pretty big opening."

You could tell that people had camped there and see that they had eaten recently. You could walk up to the edge of the opening and look out over the Okanagan Lake and see everything. You could see anyone coming from any direction. But take a few steps backwards and you could not see nor could anyone see you. The camp was far enough back that the wind would take any smoke up and away from the edge of the clearing. You were virtually undetectable in that spot.

Then it hit him. There is only one kind of person that would have picked such a spot, and for the very reasons just mentioned. Yes, outlaws were here and they would be back. Dad told his friend and after very little discussion they left in on big hurry! It scared dad and he said if he or his friend told anyone of the incident someone would tell someone and then they may be the reason for the next funeral, theirs!

Dad was still reluctant to tell the story even after these many years, and you know, I kinda know why. There were outlaws then that took very little consideration in killing someone that would reveal their secret.

I cannot leave without telling you some Okanogan Indian Stories. These three are traditional ones that you can relate to. I have heard stories that I had a hard time listening to and then trying to understand. I hope you enjoy them. And **"The Way I Heard It"**:

"Story of Coyote as a Beautiful Woman"

Coyote [*Sin-ka'-lip*] and his brother Fox [*Why-ay'-looh*] were living in their tepee alone. They were very hungry. They hunted and continued to hunt, but without success. Each sundown they failed; each sundown they returned to their lodge, tired, empty-handed and more hungry than ever. At last Fox gave up hope. He left Coyote and went to another country in search of food.

Coyote remained at home, starving and scheming. Always hungry, he ate everything he could find, from insects to leaves. At last he got an idea that would bring him food. Nearby was a great encampment of people who hated him. He thought to fool these people and obtain something to stay his growing hunger.

In the encampment was a fine looking young warrior named Badger [*E-whe-whoot'-ken*], living with his four sisters, who loved their brother, Badger. Badger killed plenty of game, generously giving meat to all the poor. Many of the old wanted him for a son-in-law, but Badger did not fancy any of the maidens among his own people. He wished to find a wife in a far country.

One very sunny day, when the Badger's sisters went for their daily bath, they saw a beautiful, strange woman sitting on the river bank painting her face with fine, and many-colored paints. The sisters were pleased. They asked the stranger to come to their tepee. They hoped that their warrior brother might accept her as a wife.

When Badger reached home from hunting, he was attracted by the strange woman. He asked her to his special seat in the big tepee, accorded only to a wife. She accepted shyly, but that night refused to sleep with Badger. She said to him, "Before I can take you as a husband, I must carry home four loads of food for my parents. And each trip your sisters must go with me, all carrying packages of dried meat."

To this Badger agreed, and the next day the five women carried four loads each to the tepee for the supposed old parents. The handsome woman was Coyote [*Sin-ka'-lip*] himself, who made the four sisters wait while he went alone with the food inside the tepee. He told the sisters that the old people did not want to see strangers, pretended to hold talk with the parents, mimicking the voices of the old people.

When Coyote had all the food stored, he ran away from Badger's sisters, turning himself back into his old self, the old Coyote [*Sin-ka'-lip*]. To save their brother's pride, the sisters kept secret Coyote's trick. But a few sundown's later when Badger went to the sweat-house where some men were ahead of him, he heard them say:

"There comes the proud and handsome Badger, he who refused the good women of his own people, who had Coyote for a wife. We do not want to sweat-house with him."

This angered Badger, and he was very ashamed. And after chasing Coyote from the country, he humbled himself to his people and took from among them a wife. Badger has ever since been humble among the animals and the animal people and you see very seldom the Badger. He does not like people to see him.

"Mosquito"

Once there lived four brothers who had a small brother, who was very lazy and greedy for blood. When the older brothers did any killing, he was given the blood, which he devoured without cooking. Each night this little boy, Mosquito [*Sch'-lux*], was sent to the sweat-house with the medicine bag to hunt for *shoo'-mesh* power.

One night as he drew near the sweat-house, he heard voices whispering. Thinking it was the enemy; he ran home and told the story, what he had heard. Mosquito was whipped and sent back to the sweat-house for the night. He sneaked and crawled into the sweat-house to cry himself to sleep.

Far in the night, before the day came, little Mosquito heard the (death) cries of his brothers. Soon the enemy came to the sweat-house to kill him. They stabbed with their tomahawks in the darkness of the sweat-house, and Mosquito put red paint on the tips of the weapons. The enemy, believing this to be blood, went away, leaving the little orphaned boy alone.

After the sun trailed high, Mosquito went to the teepee only to find his dead brothers. Mosquito was sad. Crying, he went to the river and made himself a canoe. He floated down the river wailing, lamenting, singing his song for the dead, "*O-o-h-la-lute, Cooh pa-pools en la kitchs*! (O-oh,n-no. They k-killed my brothers!)."

Mosquito boy went a long ways; and as he turned a curve in the river, he saw a great encampment of people. They called to him to come and eat chokecherries. But Mosquito told them that he did not eat chokecherries, and with all their coaxing he would not stop.

Mosquito had gone another long ways when he came in sight of a second encampment of people. They called to him, "Come here! Come here Mosquito! Come and eat *Ol-la-la*!"

Mosquito answered back, "Ohh la-lute! (Oh no!)." Mosquito, little boy, floated on, singing in sorrow, "*Ooh! Cooh pa-pools en la kitchs*!"

Mosquito drifted on, crying his song of sadness. He came to another encampment of many people. They said, "There comes Mosquito! He likes blood. Call to him to come and eat." The people called to him to come, but he refused.

Mosquito floated on, singing his song for the dead. The people told him that the blood was not cooked; and then he slowly turned his canoe in mid-stream and came ashore. Making sure that his canoe would not float away, he went to the feast. While he was eating, the people pushed his canoe adrift, and it was carried on the water. The people told Mosquito that his canoe was gone.

Mosquito boy ran to catch his canoe, but his stomach was full. He could not run fast, and in his haste he tripped and fell. A stick pierced through his stomach, letting out all the blood. From the wound a little fly flew away, lighting on a cottonwood tree close by. The little fly sang, "*Ohh! Cooh pa-pools en la kitchs!*"

The people heard the song and said to the little fly, "When the future generations come, you will sing your song for the dead. You will live on the blood of men, on the blood of people who caused the death of your brothers. It will be your revenge."

And to this day the little fly, Mosquito, glories in sucking the blood of men in revenge for the death of his four brothers.

"Rattlesnake Kills Salmon"

Salmon's lodge was in the midst of the cliffs of the Swah-netk'-qha waterfalls. He was a great warrior and one sun heard of a beautiful virgin whom the warriors were trying to win as a wife. Salmon [En'-tee-tuek] traveled to Kalispell country to find her. When he reached the tribe, he made war on the people, stole the girl, and brought her to his cliff dwelling.

Salmon lived in happiness with his wife. She loved his handsome face, red of color. This angered people. They became mad at him. All the warriors sought to kill Salmon, but all alike failed. They could not reach him in his cliff lodge above the roaring falls of the big river.

Rattlesnake [Hah-ah-ooh-lah] was an old man who lived close by the cliff where Salmon resided. He soon envied his neighbor, Salmon. He began to make arrows, singing as he worked. He finished one arrow on which he had worked for several sundown's. Rattlesnake stepped outside his bough-covered lodge and shot Salmon through the head. Rattlesnake went back into his lodge while Salmon fell from the cliff and floated away on the river.

Salmon's wife, crying for her husband, was soon carried away by Salmon's strongest rivals. These were the four Wolf brothers [En-ze'-chen]. They took her to their own teepee where she had to work, watched always by the other wives of the Wolf brothers.

Salmon's body continued down the big river carried a long distance by the high waters. As the water grew less in depth, Salmon's body landed on dry land where soon only his backbone remained in the hot sun. One sun as Mouse [Gou'-kouh-ana] and her sister were hunting for something to steal; they came upon the remains of her Chief, Salmon. Taking the bones, Mouse stole fish and salmon oil from an encampment of people close by, and doctored Salmon. She greased his backbone till the flesh began to grow. Mouse worked hard to bring life back to her master, her Chief.

It was many sundown's before Salmon was able to get up, sound and well from the helping hands of Mouse. But, finally, he was strong and started for home.

When he reached the *Swah-netk'-qha*, he could not find his wife. He went to his neighbor, Rattlesnake, to inquire about her, to know where she had gone. Salmon heard Rattlesnake singing, "*T-pin' tina, kis-na-lee'-ah*! (I shot him, and he ran down the cliffs!). Rattlesnake continued, "I shot him! He was Chief, but he is Chief no more."

Salmon entered the lodge of Rattlesnake. Rattlesnake pretended that he was crying was mourning for the death of Salmon. Salmon did not speak. He took a piece of the burning firewood, went outside of the dry-boughed lodge, and set it afire. Soon Rattlesnake was burned to death. From his eye there crawled a small snake of the rattler. This was Rattlesnake's *shoo'-mesh* power. Salmon said to it, "You will always crawl on your breast. It is a revenge for Rattlesnake killing me."

Salmon went on his way. He soon found his wife, held by the Wolf tribe. He killed all the Wolf brothers but the youngest. He sent young Wolf to the timber, to make his home in hiding. Salmon took his wife back to the *Swah-netk'qha.* He left his cliff home, left it for the water. There he was much safer from his many rivals among the land people.

The flint point of the arrow with which Rattlesnake shot Salmon stuck fast in Salmon's head. It has remained there ever since, where it can be found even to this day. When we eat the soup made of the salmon's head, where we find the arrow right between the eyes of the head of the salmon, you can find that today.

Glenny ANM

These next stories are of people you should know, or I know, or you should learn more about.

The first one is about my brother Glenny. When he was born the doctors said he had a problem, they called it "mongoloid". The immigration people at the border in Oroville were very adamant about not allowing him into America. He was born in Penticton and we lived in Omak.

The immigration people argued for two long hours with Dad and Mom, they said "take him back to Penticton let him live his life out there, they don't live much past a year anyway." And the argument went on and on and on, finally Mom said "God gave me my baby and we will live with him as long as He wishes." For some reason that was enough, they let them through the border, and my brother came home.

He lived healthy, happy and always had a smile and a glad handshake for everyone he met... And the doctors kept saying the same thing, "that he will die soon." Dad and Mom would hear none of this and took Glenny on fewer and fewer trips to the doctors.

None of the family was surprised at his health or his happiness through the years. He was like Mom and Dad, a person that was always there to say hello, give you a smile and make you feel good and give you a big handshake if you needed it.

Dad passed in 2003, Mom passed in 2006, and Glenny passed in 2010; he was 60 years old.

This is what was on his Memorial Folder:

His progress may seem very slow,
Accomplishments he may not show
And he'll require extra care
From the folks he meets way down there..

He may not run or laugh or play;
His thoughts may seem quite far away.
In many ways he won't adapt.
And he'll be known as handicapped.

So let's be careful where he's sent,
We want his life to be content.
Please, Lord, find parents who
Will do a special job for you

They will not realize right away
The leading role they're asked to play.
But with this child sent from above
Comes stronger faith and richer Love.

And soon they'll know the privilege given
In caring for this gift from Heaven
Their precious charge, so meek, so mild
Is Heaven's very special child.

My Brother Glenny

Len Marchand ANM

I cannot say enough about Len, though we know each other as relatives, I have always admired him as a man, a great man, and a role model for First Nations People to emulate. He and my brother Clifford used to run around together when they were young. Clifford spoke little of that time, but was always proud to say he really knew Len.

His story, "Breaking Trail" by Len Marchand and Matt Hughes is one every Indian should read. Especially the older ones so they can see not how hard things were, but how they can be overcome. I have heard so many older Indians talk of their hard times, and rightly so, but look at how they have been overcome by study and hard work.

He got a Master's Degree in Forestry and on his way to a PhD, became involved in the North American Indian Brotherhoods' fight for full citizenship for his people. He became the first Indian special assistant to the Federal minister responsible for Indian Affairs. He became the first Indian elected to the House of Commons, and the first of his People to become a Minister of the Crown.

My Father was so very proud of the book he received from Len, he was not a boasting man, but he showed everyone in our family and every Indian he knew. I could see the pride he had in Len, and I too am proud to say he is a relative and that I know him.

Clarence Louie ANM

Chief Clarence Louie, CEO of the Osoyoos Indian Band Development Corporation (OIBDC), has 450 Band Members and operates 10 companies with over 500 employees on the Reserve. There are 31 Bands from throughout Canada and America represented among the employees.

He has been awarded the Order of B.C., May 2006, the Aboriginal Achievement Award in April 2004, recognized by MacLean's Magazine as one of the top 50 Canadians to watch in 2003, and the Ernest & Young Social Entrepreneur of the year 2008.

He is a man I can say that I know and that I truly admire. If you ever have an opportunity to meet with him or listen to him speak you will know your time was well spent. He is a great leader and the Osoyoos Indian Band should be proud of them for having the wisdom to continue to have him as their leader.

I have come to the end of this journey and found I had left so much out and not shown you pictures of so many things. My hope is that you have enjoyed this offering of stories and have got something from them. Thank you for taking the time and the hope is that you keep reading and learning.

26084798R00148

Made in the USA
Charleston, SC
22 January 2014